The Osumi Islands
Culture, Society, Industry and Nature

**Kagoshima University
Research Center for the Pacific Islands**

Cover Design: Ryuta TERADA

The Osumi Islands

Culture, Society, Industry and Nature

Edited by
Kei KAWAI, Ryuta TERADA and Sueo KUWAHARA

Yaku-shima Island. Photo: Ryuta TERADA

Kagoshima University Research Center for the Pacific Islands

© Kagoshima University Research Center for the Pacific Islands (KURCPI) 2017

First published: March 2017

Kagoshima University Research Center for the Pacific Islands
   1-21-24 Korimoto, Kagoshima City, 890-8580 Japan
   Phone +81 99 285 7394
   Fax   +81 99 285 6197

All rights reserved. No part of this publication may be reproduced or transmitted in any form or by any means without prior written permission from the publisher. Copyrights of the photos are held by the photographers.

For bibliographic purposes this book should be cited as follows:
Kei KAWAI, Ryuta TERADA and Sueo KUWAHARA (eds.) 2017. The Osumi Islands: Culture, Society, Industry and Nature. Hokuto Shobo Publishing, Tokyo. xii + 108 pages; 26.6 cm.
Published on 10 March, 2017. Publisher: Hokuto Shobo Publishing.

ISBN 978-4-89290-041-9

Technical editing, graphic design and DTP: Ryuta TERADA

The Kagoshima University Research Center for the Pacific Islands (KURCPI) focuses on the studies on island-zones in Kagoshima, Oceania and its surroundings. An island-zone, consisting of an area that encompasses a group of islands, is a space where networks of people, things and information are formed and interaction among islands take place. An aggregation of island-zones comprises an island-sphere.
    The KURCPI aims to promote interdisciplinary studies on islands and islands zones in Oceania and its surroundings. The results of the studies are combined to promote comprehensive understanding of islands and islands zones and to further the welfare of people in Oceania and its surroundings.
KURCPI website. http://cpi.kagoshima-u.ac.jp/index.html

Printed in Japan

Contents

Notes on Contributors vi
Preface viii
Map of islands in Kagoshima ix
Various Views in the Osumi Islands xi

Part I Culture and Society
1. **Culture and Society in the Osumi Islands**
   Sueo KUWAHARA 2
2. **Tourism in the Osumi Islands: Focusing on Yaku-shima and Tanega-shima Islands**
   Sueo KUWAHARA 5
3. **Current Conditions and Future Deployment of Broadband Services on Kuchinoerabu-jima Island**
   Masato MASUYA 11
4. **Demographical Structure and Social Changes of the Villages in the Osumi Islands
   – Reclamation, Migration, Extinction, Creation and Cultural Renaissance –**
   Shunsuke NAGASHIMA 21
5. **Beginning of Food Production in the Osumi Archipelago**
   Hiroto TAKAMIYA and Naoko NAKAMURA 27

Part II Industry
6. **Profile of Industries in Tanega-shima, Yaku-shima and Mishima-mura**
   Satoru NISHIMURA 38
7. **Background and Future Prospects of the Efforts toward the Introduction of *Yokowa* (young bluefin tuna) Trolling by the Yaku-shima Fisheries Cooperative Association**
   Takashi TORII 40
8. **Fruit Trees on Tanega-shima and Yaku-shima**
   Masashi YAMAMOTO 45
9. **Medicinal Plants of Tanega-shima and Yaku-shima Islands**
   Sota YAMAMOTO 50

Part III Nature
10. **Trends in Natural Science Research on the Osumi Islands**
    Kei KAWAI 70
11. **Review of the Ichthyofauna of Yaku-shima Island in the Osumi Islands, Southern Japan, with 15 New Records of Marine Fishes**
    Hiroyuki MOTOMURA 74
12. **Review of the Hydrothermal Crab, *Xenograpsus testudinatus* Ng, Huang & Ho, 2000 (Crustacea: Decapoda: Brachyura: Xenograpsidaae) Inhabiting the Adjacent Waters of the Satsunann Islands, Southern Japan**
    Hiroshi SUZUKI, Tatsuki IWASAKI, Yu UTSUNOMIYA and Amami IWAMOTO 81
13. **Study on the Marine Natural Products Chemistry of the Red Alga, *Hanayanagi*, in the Osumi Islands**
    Toshiyuki HAMADA, Satoaki ONITSUKA and Hiroaki OKAMURA 89
14. **Geological Overview of the Shimanto Belt in Tanega-shima Island**
    Yujin KITAMURA, Naoya SAKAMOTO and Kuniyo KAWABATA 95
15. **Black Fly of the Osumi Islands**
    Yasushi OTSUKA 99
16. **Seaweeds and Coastal Environment in the Osumi Islands**
    Ryuta TERADA and Yuki WATANABE 104

Notes on Contributors

Editors

Kei KAWAI is a professor at the Research Center for the Pacific Islands, Kagoshima University. He specializes in marine biology and has conducted fieldwork in the islands of the Pacific and Kagoshima.

Ryuta TERADA is a professor at the United Graduate School of Agricultural Sciences, Kagoshima University. His scientific interests are in the biodiversity of marine plants including coastal ecosystems, and in the sustainable utilization of seaweed resources worldwide.

Sueo KUWAHARA is a professor of anthropology at Kagoshima University. He has conducted fieldwork in Malaysia over a number of years and more recently commenced research on the culture(s) of Japan's southwestern archipelago.

Contributors

Toshiyuki HAMADA is an associate professor of Organic Chemistry in the Graduate School of Science and Engineering, Kagoshima University. He has worked on isolation, structure elucidation and functional analysis of bioactive substances derived from marine invertebrates and medical plants.

Amami IWAMOTO was a student in Faculty of Fisheres, Kagoshima University. She specialized in marine biology.

Tatsuki IWASAKI was a student in Graduate School of Fisheries, Kagoshima University. He specialized in life history of marine crab.

Kuniyo KAWABATA is a JSPS research fellow in Department of Earth and Environmental Sciences, Graduate School of Science and Engineering, Kagoshima University. She is specialized in geology, material seismology and fluid geochemistry.

Yujin KITAMURA is an assistant professor in Department of Earth and Environmental Sciences, Graduate School of Science and Engineering, Kagoshima University. He is specialized in geology and forensic geology.

Masato MASUYA is a professor of Computing and Communications Center, Kagoshima University. His research interests include protein tertiary structure prediction and Information Communication Technology utilization.

Hiroyuki MOTOMURA is a professor of Ichthyology in the Kagoshima University Museum. He has worked on systematics and biogeography of marine and freshwater fishes in the Indo-Pacific region.

Shunsuke NAGASHIMA is a professor emeritus of Nissology on Human Life and Environment, including Humanities and Social Sciences at Kagoshima University. He has conducted fieldwork in almost all Japanese Archipelagoes and island nations since the 1970's.

Naoko NAKAMURA is a professor in the Research Center for Archeology, Kagoshima University. She is specialized in archaeology. She has been working on prehistory of Kyusyu, the Osumi Islands and the Amami Islands.

Satoru NISHIMURA is a professor of Economics at Kagoshima University. He has conducted research on land tenure systems in the Philippines since 1990. He has recently extended his areas of research to Fiji and Federal States of Micronesia.

Hiroaki OKAMURA is a professor of Organic Chemistry in the Graduate School of Science and Engineering, Kagoshima University. He has worked on design and synthesis of bioactive organic compounds and functional materials.

Satoaki ONITSUKA is an assistant professor of Organic Chemistry in the Graduate School of Science and Engineering, Kagoshima University. He is majoring in synthetic organic chemistry. His research interests include the development of functional materials in both catalysis and sensing.

Yasushi OTSUKA is an associate professor in the Research Center for the Pacific Islands, Kagoshima University. He specializes in medical zoology, and has conducted researches on blackfly and mosquito in Asia and Micronesia.

Naoya SAKAMOTO is a graduate student in Department of Earth and Environmental Sciences, Faculty of Science, Kagoshima University. He studies geology and has conducted fieldwork in the Tanega-shima island.

Hiroshi SUZUKI is a professor of Faculty of Fisheries, Kagoshima University. He has worked on systematics, ecology and biogeography of marine and freshwater crustacean decapods.

Hiroto TAKAMIYA is a professor in the Research Center for the Pacific Islands, Kagoshima University. He is specialized in prehistoric anthropology. He has been working on prehistory of the Central Ryukyus (Amami and Okinawa Archipelagos).

Takashi TORII is an associate professor of Faculty of Fisheries, Kagoshima University. He specializes in fisheries and economics, and has conducted fieldwork in the islands of Fiji and Kagoshima.

Yu UTSUNOMIYA is a student in Graduate School of Fisheries, Kagoshima University. He specializes in fisheries and marine biology and has conducted fieldwork on life history of marine crab.

Yuki WATANABE is a Ph.D student at Kagoshima University and the Research Fellow of Japan Society for the Promotion of Science (JSPS). His specialty is the biodiversity and eco-physiology of macro-algae.

Masashi YAMAMOTO is a professor of Faculty of Agriculture, Kagoshima University. He specialized in fruit tree science and has conducted fieldwork in the islands of the Pacific and Kagoshima.

Sota YAMAMOTO is an associate professor in the Research Center for the Pacific Islands, Kagoshima University. He specializes in ethnobotany and tropical agriculture. His current interests include crop diversity, distribution, and dispersal routes in Asia and Oceania.

Preface

Kagoshima is an island prefecture and has the second-largest number of islands in Japan. The distance between the northernmost and southernmost borders of Kagoshima is approximately 600 kilometers. The islands in Kagoshima are primarily located in the sub-tropical zone. Kagoshima prefecture has 605 islands, 28 of which are residential.

The Kagoshima University Research Center for the Pacific Islands (KURCPI) published books in 2015 and 2016 entitled *The Islands of Kagoshima, 2nd edition*, and *The Amami islands*, respectively. The Islands of Kagoshima comprise the islands of Koshiki, Osumi, Tokara, and Amami. The Project Planning Committee at KURCPI plans to publish this book series in English to generate global awareness of these remarkable islands. Next, we will introduce the Osumi Islands.

The Osumi Islands are located north of the Ryukyu Archipelago that stretch southwest from Kagoshima to Taiwan. The Osumi Islands consist of Yaku-shima, Tanega-shima, Take-shima, Kuro-shima, Io-jima, Shōwa Iō-jima, Mage-shima, and Kuchinoerabu-jima. Yaku-shima, which is the largest of the Osumi Islands, was registered as a World Natural Heritage Site in 1993 because of its high biodiversity. After this registration, many tourists visited the island. Because the landscapes of the islands of Take-shima, Kuro-shima, and Io-jima were very unique, they were registered by Japanese Geo-parks. On the other hands, Tanega-shima, which is the second-largest island, was the area where the Jesuit priest Francis Xavier landed in 1551. Therefore, the Osumi Islands have diversity from the natural, cultural, economic, and social points of view.

To conclude, we would like to thank the Project Planning Committee members, Kagoshima University, the Kagoshima local government, the public office on each island, and the local islanders for their support. We hope this book will help people come to know about the Islands of Kagoshima.

Kei KAWAI

Director
Research Center for the Pacific Islands
Kagoshima University

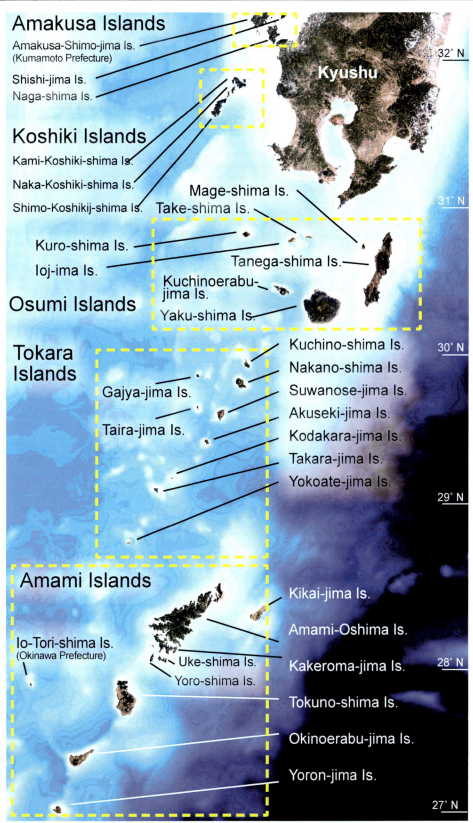

Map of the Islands in Kagoshima

Right Photos: Various Views in the Osumi Islands.

A–F: Various landscapes in the Osumi Islands. **A**, Take-shima Island; **B**, Io-jima Island; **C**, Kuro-shima Island; **D**, Kuchinoerabu-jima Island; **E**, Yaku-shima Island; **F**, JAXA Tanegashima Space Center in Tanega-shima Island.

G–J: Infrastructures in the Osumi Islands. **G**, NTT West's Tashiro Wireless Linking Station at Kuchinoerabu-shima Island; **H**, Arrival of the municipal ferry boat, *Ferry Mishima*, in Io-jima Island, Mishima Village; **I**, Local inhabitants who say goodbye to their friends on board in Io-jima Island. The arrival and departure of the ferry boat is one of the most important event in daily life; **J**, Kanagatake municipal elementary / junior high school in Kuchinoerabu-jima Island.

K–O: Nature and agriculture in the Osumi Islands. **K**, *Chikura-no-iwaya* (literally, cave of thousand seats), a sea cave located in the east coast of Tanega-shima Island appears at low tide with a series of halls and corridors networked in the Neogene sandstone mound along the beach; **L**, An underwater view of the hot spring near the Showa Io-jima Island; **M**, A marine red alga, *Chondria armata* that contains the doimoic acid. Domoic acid is a kainic acid analog neurotoxin that causes amnesic shellfish poisoning; **N**, *Citrus tankan* (Tankan in Japanese) in Yaku-shima Island; **O**, Sugarcane field in Tanega-shima Island.

Photos: Ryuta TERADA (B, D, E, F, I, J, M, O), Hiroshi SUZUKI (A, C, L), Masato MASUYA (G), Kei KAWAI (H), Yujin KITAMURA (K), Masashi YAMAMOTO (N).

Various Views in the Osumi Islands

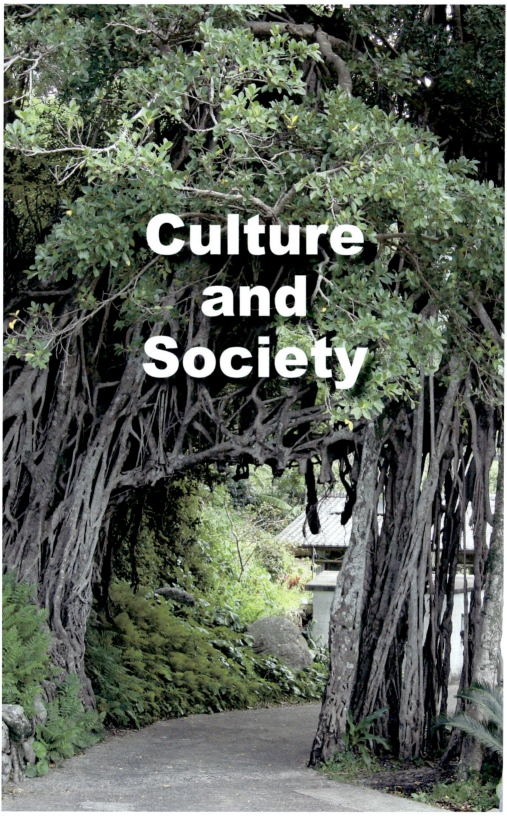

Banyan tree (*Gajumaru* in Japanese), *Ficus microcarpa* at Shitogo, Yaku-shima Island. Photo: Ryuta TERADA

Chapter 1
Culture and Society in the Osumi[1] Islands

Sueo KUWAHARA

1. The Osumi Islands

The Osumi Islands are located to the south of the Osumi Peninsula of Kagoshima Prefecture. In a narrow sense, the archipelago consists of 4 islands: Tanega-shima, Yaku-shima, Kuchinoerabu-jima, and Mage-shima. However, in a wider sense, it comprises 3 further islands, which form Mishima Village: Take-shima, Iō-jima, and Kuro-shima.

Mage-shima was an inhabited island before the Second World War, but after the war it became deserted. Municipally, the island belongs to Nishinoomote city of Tanega-shima. The largest island in the Osumi Islands is Yaku-shima. Among these 7 islands, Io-jima and Kuchinoerabu-jima are active volcanic islands. Moreover, there was a large eruption in Kuchinoerabu-jima as recent as 29th May 2015, and all the islanders were forced to evacuate to the neighboring island of Yaku-shima because of the pyroclastic flow. However, almost one year later, the islanders were able to return home after the evacuation order was lifted.

Historically, and dating from the early 9th century, Yaku-shima and Tanega-shima comprised a single district called "Taneto". However, the two islands were incorporated into the Osumi Province of the Osumi peninsula. In the early 13th century, Tokinobu Higo, the founding ancestor of Tanega-shima, was given the 12 islands of Tanega-shima, Yaku-shima, Kuchinoerabu-jima, Iō-jima, Take-shima and the 7 Tokara Islands, and established his rule over the islands. In the mid-16th century, firearms were introduced into Tanega-shima by Portuguese sailors, which was the first introduction to Japan and a very important event in the nation's history. Yaku-shima had been put under the rule of the Tanega-shima clan, but in the mid-16th century the island was temporarily occupied by the Nejime clan of Osumi Province. Also, at the end of the 16th century, Yaku-shima, Tanega-shima, and Kuchinoerabu-jima became the territory of the -shimazu Clan, but were returned to the Tanega-shima Clan soon after (Yaku-shima Kyodoshi Hensan Iinkai ed. 2003: 18-20, Nakatane-cho Kyodoshi Hensan Iinkai ed. 1970: 6).

Each island in the Osumi Islands has a unique and individualistic culture. Tanega-shima is located 40 km to the southeast of the mainland of Kagoshima prefecture, and about 115 km from Kagoshima city. The island stretches 25 km from north to south, and 8 km from east to west, with the highest point 282 m above sea level. The population is about 31,000 (2010 census)[2]. The island is known as an island where firearms were first introduced to Japan, and it has subsequently established a gun museum, gun festival, and blacksmith industry. In 1969, a Space Center was established on Tanega-shima, and a number of rockets have been launched from the site, which has become a center of Japanese space development[3].

Mage-shima is a flat island located 12 km to the west of Tanega-shima and has highest point of 71 m. The island is surrounded by rich fishing grounds. Before the war, the island had

---

1) There are two types of spelling for the "Osumi" Islands, that is, the "Ohsumi" Islands and the "Osumi" Islands. Here, the "Osumi (Ōsumi)" will be used.
2) Kagoshima "shima" no sapōta: http://www.shima-supporter.com/islands/tane-yaku/
3) JAXA: http://www.jaxa.jp/about/centers/tnsc/
4) Nishinoomote-shi: http://www.city.nishinoomote.lg.jp/admin/gyousei/shoukai/gaiyou/1307.html
5) Yaku-shima-cho: http://www.town.Yaku-shima.kagoshima.jp/about-Yaku-shima/introduction/
6) Yaku-shima-cho: http://www.town.Yaku-shima.kagoshima.jp/about-Yaku-shima/introduction/

only been used as a fishery base by Tangega-shima's fishermen who stayed there for about one to two months during the fishing season for flying fish. There were no residents. After the war, in the 1950s, agricultural development groups settled in the island. At a peak period in 1959, 528 people with 113 households lived on the island and grew sugar cane and ran a dairy farm. However, islanders gradually left and finally the island became deserted in March 1980. Currently, the majority of the land has been acquired by a private company[4].

Yaku-shima is located 60 km to the southeast of mainland Kagoshima prefecture and 18 km to the west of Tanega-shima. It is the largest island in the Osumi Islands with a land area of about 500 square kilometers. There are many high mountains in Yaku-shima, including Miyanouradake (1,936 m), the highest mountain in Kyushu, and thus Yaku-shima is called "an alps on the sea". Ninety percent of the island is covered with forest and cedar trees called "Yakusugi" that are more than 1000 years old. One fifth of the island is registered as World Natural Heritage[5], through which ecotourism has been very popular.

Kuchinoerabu-jima is a volcanic island located 12 km to the west of Yaku-shima, and its land area is 38 square kilometers. Municipally, the island belongs to Yaku-shima Town and the population is 152 (2010 census). It is still fresh in the minds of islanders that Mt. Shindake erupted and all residents were forced to evacuate to Yaku-shima. There is a daily ferry service between Yaku-shima and Kuchinoerabu-jima.

The three islands of Take-shima, Iō-jima, and Kuro-shima, which municipally form Mishima Village, are located 40 km to the southeast of the Satsuma Peninsula with the total land area of 31 square kilometers, and a population of about 400. The islands are active in regional promotion around Iō-jima[6].

2. Summary of this section

This section comprises four articles, which are categorized into four main themes: tourism, communication, migration, and prehistoric food production. KUWAHARA's article on the tourism of the Osumi Islands describes the current situation of tourism on the three island areas of Mishima-mura, Yaku-shima and Tanega-shima, and then the author points out that the studies on tourism in the Osumi Islands are very few with the exception of ecotourism in Yaku-shima. The second part of his research discusses tourism of Yaku-shima and Tanega-shima from a comparative perspective, and then discussed tourism of the two island areas and Mishima-mura. The author points out that tourism in these three island areas has been developed on an individual island based, and there are almost no tourism links between the three island areas.

MASUYA's article is on the deployment of broadband services in a small remote island of Kuchinoerabu-jima with a population of only 122. The author first describes in detail the current situation of the telecommunication environment by examining fixed-line communication services and mobile communication services on the island and points out that the telecommunication environment is 20 years behind that of the mainland. The author then describes underwater optical cable lines, wireless links and satellite connections as the future deployment of a broadband environment, and suggests LTE mobile communication services provided by mobile telecommunication carriers as the best and easiest method for the island to build relevant communication networks.

NAGASHIMA describes the population movements and the history of migration in Yaku-shima, Kuchinoerabujma, Mage-shima, and Tanega-shima, and points out that the Osumi Islands are demographically significant because of their diversity. However, the author also points out the lack of documentation about these islands. The author then discusses the significance of the organizational and systematic preservation of the local records, and also the resources collected and maintained by the islanders that are not public. He emphasizes the importance of the scope for university researchers to collaborate and make such resources accessible to the wider public and scholarly communities.

In their paper, TAKAMIYA and NAKAMURA review

previous studies on the beginning of food production in mainland southern Kyushu and the Amami Islands in order to understand the origin of agriculture in the Osumi Islands. The authors suggest that food production began in the Osumi Islands somewhere between the early Yayoi period (c.10th century BC) and the 10th century AD. The authors then introduce the latest evidence from Tanega-shima and suggest the possibility of food production in the Osumi Islands of prehistoric time.

Chapter 2
Tourism in the Osumi Islands: Focusing on Yaku-shima and Tanega-shima Islands

Sueo KUWAHARA

1. Introduction

What is the current situation of tourism in the Osumi Islnads of Kagoshima Prefecture, which comprise Tanega-shima, Yaku-shima, Kuchinoerabu-jima and the three islands of Mishima-mura village (Take-shima, Io-jima, Kuro-shima)? The information on tourism of Yaku-shima, which is known as a World Natural Heritage site, is abundant, but the tourism information on the other islands is little known.

The major features of tourism in the Osumi Islands would be that not like some islands of Okinawa and Izu, they did not experience mass tourism which was the major characteristic of tourism in 1970s and 1980s. Mass tourism was promoted in many places in Japan as a new tourism industry, but in the 1990s new tourism industries such as green tourism, ecotourism and so on were born as alternative ventures[1].

How have these various tourism industries been developed in the islands of Kagoshima, especially in the Osumi Islands? This article first describes briefly the current situation of tourism in the Osumi Islands, and then discusses the features and the future prospects of the Osumi Islands by focusing on tourism in Tanega-shima and Yaku-shima, and comparing them.

2. Tourism of the Osumi Islands

2.1. Tourism of Mishima-mura village

Mishima-mura village of Kagoshima District consists of the three islands of Take-shima, Io-jima, and Kuro-shima. The population of Mishima-mura village is 388 with 213 households (as of December 2016, Mishima-mura Municipal Village Office). There is no high school in the village, and the decrease of the labor force is continuing. As a way out of the situation, Mishima-mura village has put much effort into developing the livestock industry as well as tourism.

Take-shima, which is the nearest island to Kagoshima City among the three islands of Mishima-mura village, is located 94 km to the south of Kagoshima City or 3 hours by ferry from Kagoshima port. Its circumference is 9.7 km and the land area is 4.2 square kilometers. The island is flat in shape with the highest point about 220 meters. The population is 81 with 47 households (as of 2016, Mishima-mura Municipal Village Office), and the major industry is livestock farming. The bamboo shoots from the rich bamboo forest that covers the whole island are also processed as a speciality of the village and sold as a souvenir[2].

Satsuma Io-jima is located 14 km to the west of Take-shima and about 40 minutes by ferry from Take-shima. The circumference and land area are 14.5 km and 11.7 square kilometers respectively. The highest point is 703 meters, Mt. Io-dake, which is an active volcano. The population is 124

---

1) The word "alternative tourism" has been used as a comprehensive word that includes a new way of tourism which is alternative to mass tourism. Recently, the word "sustainable tourism" has more often been used. This word is based on the concept of "sustainable development" that takes environmental issues into consideration. The diversification of tourism seems to be in progress such as mass tourism, alternative tourism, sustainable tourism, heritage tourism, industrial tourism, historical tourism, cultural tourism, green tourism, educational tourism, community tourism, ethnic tourism, contents tourism, geo tourism, and so on (Tomimoto 2015).
2) Mishima-mura Municipal Village Hall: http://mishimamura.com/tourism/419/ (referred on 16 December 2016).

with 62 households (as of 2016, Mishima-mura Municipal Village Office). The major industries are livestock farming and fisheries, and tourism is also promoted by utilizing the hot springs and historic sites. The seawater of the island is turned to yellow-green and red in color because of the hot springs and sulfur which flow from the volcano (Fig. 1). Io-jima is also well-known as an island where the famous Buddhist monk Shunkan died in exile in the late 12 century. There are a lot of historical sites related to him on the island. Shunkan is also known in the story of a Kabuki play. In 1996, the kabuki actor Nakamura Kankurō acted Shunkan on the beach of Io-jima, by which the island became well-known. The island is also known as the place where Emperor Antoku, who was said to have died in the Battle of Dannoura between the Genji clan and the Heike clan, escaped and survived. There are some historical sites and records of the emperor on the island. The company, Yamaha Resort, built an airport with a runway of 600 meters in length on the island in October 1973, and opened a resort hotel there in April 1974. However, the airport and hotel were shut down in April 1984 because of a poor business performance[3].

Kuro-shima is located 36 kilometers to the west of Io-jima or about one hour distance by ferry. The island is 15 kilometers in circumference and 15.5 square kilometers in land area, and the largest of the three islands of Mishima-mura village. The highest point of the island is 622 meters and there are a few mountains over 500 meters. The island is mostly covered with trees and bamboo forest. There are two villages called Oosato and Katadomari. The population of the island is 175 with 98 households (as of 2016, Mishima-mura Municipal Village Office). The major industries are livestock farming and fisheries and there are some very good fishing points around the island, which attracts a lot of fishing enthusiasts. The island is also known as the location of Sawako Ariyoshi's novel, "I don't forget", of 1968. The novel was made into a movie of the same title in the same year, and was shoot on the island. An honoring monument of the novel was built on the island, which attracts a lot of interest[4].

The annual number of tourists in Mishima-mura village is between 4,000 and 7,000, and there hasn't been an extreme increase or decrease over the years. As for tourism related events of Mishima-mura village, there is the Mishima Cup Yacht race[5] which started in 1990, African djembe festival[6] (Fig. 2), which started in 1994, and in 1996 there was a Kabuki performance of Shunkan which attracted 800 people to the island.

Fig. 1. Iō-jima port.

Fig. 2. Djembe school.

---

3) *ibid.*
4) *ibid.*
5) The first race started in August 1990 and since then, about 50 boats, around 300 crews participate in the Mishima Cup Yacht Race which is held on the first Saturday of August every year. On the day of yacht race, after arriving at Io-jima from Kagoshima city, crews enjoy sightseeing on the island by islanders' cars and hot spring. Islanders cook the sea food and BBQ for the night party of the race day.

Recently, community-based tourism by the islanders, including immigrants, has been significant. One of them is the "Initiative of Mishima-mura Geopark" which started in 2012. Geopark is the place which has earth scientific resources such as a terrain and geological features as a landscape, and people there have tried to preserve and utilize such resources (Fukami and Ōkubo 2014: 33-35). Kikai Caldera Museum Room was installed as a core facility in the Mishima Development Center near Io-jima Port. As a result of deploying vigorous activities such as publishing a pamphlet titled "Make Mishima-mura Geopark" and having professional staff responsible for Geopark at the municipal village office, Mishima-mura village with three islands and the surrounding submarine caldera were approved as Japan Geopark of "Mishima-mura-Kikai Caldera Geopark" in September 2015.

As seen above, various tourism promotions were made on the three islands of Mishima-mura. The people of the islands, who attracted only fishing tourists in the past, explored various attempts of tourism promotion such as resort tourism in the 1980s, and the Mishima Cup Yacht race, djembe school and Kabuki performance of Shunkan since the 1990s. It can be said that the islanders are steadily gaining support from Mishima-mura although the scale of tourism is small.

2.2. Yaku-shima Island
2.2.1. Current situation of tourism
Yaku-shima Island is 135 km to the south of Kagoshima City, or 60 km to the south of mainland Kagoshima Prefecture. The circumference, the land area and the highest point are 132 km, 500 square kilometers and 1,936 meters (Mt. Miyanouradake) respectively. The population was about 17,000 in 1970 but from 1990 to the present it has been about 13,000 (as of 2014, Yaku-shima town hall). The island is connected to Kagoshima, Fukuoka and Osaka by air, and to Kagoshima and Tanega-shima by two ferry boats and five jetfoils. Thus, Yaku-shima is easily accessible by public transport.

The number of tourist to Yaku-shima was 110,000 to 120,000 from 1984 to 1988, but it increased rapidly to 170,000 because jetfoils were put in service between Yaku-shima and Kagoshima in 1989. Yaku-shima was registered to World Natural Heritage in 1993 and the number of tourists increased sharply again from 1994. From 1995 to 2002, the number was around 250,000 to 280,000, but it reached 300,000 for the first time in 2003. Since 2004, the number was kept around 300,000[7], and then it reached the highest of 400,000. Since then, till today, the tourist number has kept 300,000. Also, the tourist number exceeded that of Tanega-shima for the first time in 2009.

As we have seen above, the number of tourist to Yaku-shima was around 100,000 at most until the first half of the 1980s. However, there was a sharp increase after 1990, and the number reached 400,000 in 2007. Especially in these days, because of the easy traffic access by the increase in jetfoil services, package tours from Kanto area have increased. Eco-tour guides and lodging facilities are also increasing.

2.2.2. Tourism resources
The sales point of Yaku-shima's tourism is the forest of old cedar trees called Yakusugi. After Yaku-shima was registered to World Natural Heritage in 1993, the number of tourist who came to see Jomonsugi, the oldest cedar tree in Yaku-shima, increased considerably. The feature of those who enter the mountains of Yaku-shima is that almost 70% of them go to see only the Jomonsugi cedar tree. Their destination is to make a day trip to see the Jomonsugi. Fulltime eco-tour guides who explain the nature of Yaku-shima began to organize themselves in 1993 (Makita 2001: 37–39). The Liaison Council for Eco-tour guide of Yaku-shima was established in 1999, and then, Yaku-shima Guide Registration System and the Liaison Council for the Promotion

---

6) Another leading part of the nigh party is the djembe performance by the kids of Mishima-mura and Mamadhi Keta of Republic of Guinea.
7) *Yaku-shima-cho Kikaku Chosei-ka* 2012, Statistics Yaku-shima 2011, Yaku-shima-cho.

of Ecotourism in Yaku-shima Town were also established in 2006 and 2009 respectively.

Current major tourist sites of Yaku-shima are Jomonsugi, Yakusugi Land and Shiratani Unsuikyo, which attracts a lot of tourists (Fig. 3). The other tourist sites include two waterfalls of Chihiro and Ōko, Western Forest Road, and sea turtles lay eggs at Nagata village. In 2012, the Association for Promotion of Village Ecotourism of Yaku-shima was established for the purpose of the preservation of local resources, local culture and history and the local revitalization through sustainable use of the resources. Currently, a village eco-tour has been offered by local guides in 7 villages such as Yoshida, Harumaki and so on[8].

Kuchinoerabu-jima is a volcanic island which is located 12 km to the northeast of Yaku-shima, and is municipally included within Yaku-shima town. The circumference of the island is about 50 km and the land area is 38 square kilometers. The highest point is 657 meters of Furudake. The population is 152 with 82 households (2010 National Census). The island is connected to Yaku-shima once a day (or one round service in daytime) by ferry which is run by the town[9]. It is still fresh in our mind that the islanders were forced to evacuate to Yaku-shima because of the pyroclastic flow by the big explosion of Mt.Shindake (626 m) in May 2015. Now, most of the islanders have returned to the island, and there are some tourists for fishing and hot springs, and some eco-tours are provided by islanders.

2.3. Tanega-shima

Fig. 3. Shiratani Unsuikyo of Yaku-shima.

2.3.1. Current situation of tourism

Tanega-shima is located 115 km to the south of Kagoshima city, and 40 km from the southernmost of mainland Kagoshima Prefecture. The land area and circumference are 444 square kilometers and 186 km respectively, and it is the third largest island next to Amami-Ōshima and Yaku-shima within the prefecture, and the tenth in Japan. The highest point is only 282 m, which contrasts markedly to that of Yaku-shima (1,936m). The population is about 33,000 (as of 2014, Nishinoomote City Hall), which is the second largest to Amami-Ōshima within the prefecture.

The number of tourist from 1984 to 1989 was around 200,000, and it reached 300,000 in 1990. Because of the introduction of a jetfoil service in 1989, the number of tourists by boat was almost twice the number who visited by air. The number of tourist who came by boat was more than 200,000, and it reached the peak of 288,000. On the other hand, the number of the tourists who came by air was around 100,000 per year from 1986 to 1993, and there has been no big change. Thus, it can be said that the sharp increase of tourists was brought by the effect of the new service of jetfoils.

The number of tourist was from 300,000 and 330,000 between 1990 and 2004, but reached the highest number of 450,000 in 2007. The reason behind this was that there was a price competition of the fare between the two jetfoil companies, which eventually brought a cheaper fare. However, the tourist number decreased 100,000 a year to 300,000 in 2009, and became less than 300,000 in 2011. The statistics of 2012 shows 279,000[10]. The user of boat increased from 110,000 in 1990 to between 200,000 and 240,000 in 2004, but the number decreased to 260,000 in 2010[11]. On the other hand, the user of airplane decreased sharply from 96,000 in 1985 to 40,000

---

8) "Yaku-shima village eco-tour": http://www.Yaku-shima.jp/ (referred on 23 December 2016).
9) Kagoshima prefecture "Overview of Kuchinoerabu-jima": https://www.pref.kagoshima.jp/ac07/pr/shima/gaiyo/Yaku-shima/kuchinoerabu.html (referred on 23 December 2016).

in 2010[12].

2.3.2. Tourism resources

The main feature of tourism in Tanega-shima is its various tourism resources. Firstly, as the tourism of industry, sugar factory, shochu factory, Space Center, and blacksmith are given. Secondly, as the tourism of historical sites, the first introduction in Japan of firearms and Christianity and so on are given. As the tourism of rockets, there are tours to see the exhibition in the Space Center and to visit the rocket launching site (Fig. 4). There were more than 10 rocket liftoffs between since 2012 to 2015[13]. Hotels are always full of those who are related to rocket launching, media people and tourists during the rocket lift-off.

The other features of tourism in Tanega-shima are anime pilgrimage or contents tourism and educational tourism or school trips. Minamitane town and the Space Center became the site of some animes and attracted a lot of the anime fans.

School trips to Tanega-shima is also becoming popular these years. Tanega-shima has hosted junior and senior high school students from Niigata, Hiroshima, Kyoto and Tokyo. The number of a school amounts to 80 and 320 at the most. Especially junior high school students from Niigata prefecture has been visiting Tanega-shima every year. Tanega-shima is constantly hosting at least 4 schools a year[14].

3. Comparison of Tanega-shima and Yaku-shima

There has been a sharp contrast in every aspect of tourism between Yaku-shima and Tanega-shima. Especially, there can be seen the relationship of a dichotomy between nature and culture in many

Fig. 4. Tangega-shima Space Center .

aspects. On the other hand, there is one of the few common points in the type of tourism which is known as anime pilgrimage or contents tourism, but its content is still in contrast.

The geographic differences between the two neighboring islands is remarkable. Yaku-shima is a round island with the highest mountain of Mt. Miyanouradake (1,936 m), whereas Tangashima is a long and narrow island with the highest point of less than 300 meters. Regarding tourism, looking at the two islands from the viewpoint of tourism resources, that of Yaku-shima is nature (cedar trees, high mountains etc.), whereas that of Tanega-shima is culture (rocket base, space center, guns, blacksmith etc.).

Secondly, looking from the viewpoint of anime pilgrimage, the mossy forest of Shiratani Unsuikyo of Yaku-shima is used in Hayao Miyazaki's "Princess Mononoke", whereas Nakatane Chūō High School and the Space Center of Tanega-shima are used in the animes of "Robotics Notes"[15] and "Captain Earth" respectively. The theme of former is nature, whereas that of the latter is culture.

Thirdly, comparing from the viewpoint of local museum, the theme of Yaku-shima's museum such as Yakusugi Museum, Yaku-shima Environmental and Cultural Village Center and Sea Turtle Museum is nature, while in the case of Tanega-shima's museum such as Gun Museum and Tangegashima Space Center, the theme is culture (or science).

Lastly, from the viewpoint of what tourists

---

10) Statistics Nishinoomote 2015": http://www.city.nishinoomote.lg.jp/material/files/group/9/22858675.pdf
11) *ibid.*
12) *ibid.*
13) *ibid.*
14) *ibid.* H-2A Rocket No.21 to No.29 were lifted off. H-2B Rocket No. 3 to No.5 were also lifted off.
15) A lot of anime fans came to Tanega-shima from all over Japan. 3,000 fans are said to have visited an anime shop of Robotics Notes in two months.

expect, that of Yaku-shima is nature such as Jomonsugi, the forest of Yakusugi, sea turtles, Mt. Miyanouradake and so on, whereas that of Tangegashima is surfing, Gun Festival, Rocket Launching, anime pilgrimage and so on. The age of former is the past such as Jomon Period, whereas that of Tanega-shima is the future such as space development. The dichotomy of nature and culture is also identified in electric power, that is, Yaku-shima people are supplied hydroelectric power which symbolizes nature, whereas Tanega-shima people are supplied electricity from thermal power generation which symbolizes culture. Furthermore, Sport tourism such as Rocket Marathon[16] and education tourism such as school trips of junior and senior high school students are quite established in Tanega-shima.

4. Conclusion

In the Osumi Islands, Yaku-shima is known as the island of World Natural Heritage and ecotourism, whereas Tanega-shima is known as the island of the introduction of guns, a Space Center and a rocket base. In terms of tourism, the contrast of the two islands are remarkable in every aspect. In comparison to these two islands, the tourism of the three small islands of Mishima-mura village is exerting uniqueness and individuality with features such as a volcano, djembe performance, the Mishima Cup Yacht race and Kabuki of Shunkan, though the scale of tourism is small. In this sense, in the Osumi Islands, there can be seen a contrast not only between Yaku-shima and Tanega-shima, but also between the two big islands and Mishima-mura's small islands. That is, while the former is the contrasting types of tourism, the latter is the diversity and variety of the tourism. The contrasting tourism of Yaku-shima and Tanega-shima, and Mishima-mura's tourism which is based on the diversity and uniqueness can be said to be the features of the Osumi Islands. The tourisms of these three island areas have been clearly developed individually. There are few tourism options which link the two islands, though some school trips are planned to visit the two islands. And the tourism that links the three island areas is almost none. The tourism of the Osumi Islands would become better if the three island areas cooperate by using each other's strengths in tourism and enrich the contents of the tourism of the islands. However, before that, the future technical issues need to be solved such as traffic infrastructure.

References

Mishima-mura Village of Kagoshima Prefecture: http://mishimamura.com/tourism/419/ (in Japanese)
Mishima-mura Village of Kagoshima Prefecture:http://mishimamura.com/ech/348/ (in Japanese)
Kagoshima Prefecture "Overview of Kuchinoerabu-jima Island": https://www.pref.kagoshima.jp/ac07/pr/shima/gaiyo/Yakushima/kuchinoerabu.html (in Japanese)
SHIBASAKI, S., SAKATA, Y. and NAGATA, S. 2003. Annual number of tourist and tourism demand estimation in Yaku-shima, Tanega-shima Tourism Asscociation. http://tanekan.jp/rn.html (in Japanese)
Statistics Nishinoomote 2015 (PDF version): http://www.city.nishinoomote.lg.jp/material/files/group/9/22858675.pdf (in Japanese)
TOMIMOTO, M. 2015. Study on cultural tourism as new tourism: through the view from oppsosition to symbiosis. Bulletin of Gifu Women's University 45: 59–67 (in Japanese)
Nishinoomote city: http://www.city.nishinoomote.kagoshima.jp/ (in Japanese)
FUKAMI, S. and OOKUBO, M. 2014. People's consciousness in the promotion process of Geopark planning: a case of Mishima-mura village, Kagoshima Prefecture. Regional Environmental Studies 6: 33–45. (in Japanese)
MAKITA, K. 2001. A new economic forest utilization and its active persons: the ecotourism and climbing guide in Yaku Island. Journal of Forest Economics 47(1): 35–40. (in Japanese)
Yaku-shima-cho planning and coordination division 2013. Statistics Yaku-shima 2012, Yaku-shima-cho, Kagoshima Prefecture. (in Japanese)
Yaku-shima-cho planning and coordination division 2011. Statistics Yaku-shima 2012. Yaku-shima-cho, Kagoshima Prefecture. (in Japanese)
Yaku-shima-cho Information Statistics: http://www.Yakushima-town.jp/?page_id=308 (in Japanese)
Yaku-shima village eco-tour: http://www.Yakushima.jp/ (in Japanese)
Rocket marathon: http://rockemara.jp/index.html (in Japanese)
Robotics notes pilgrimage in Tanega-shima: http://www.m-riron.sakura.ne.jp/ibento/seitijyunrei/h25/robonojyunreianime.html (in Japanese)

---

16) The 30th Rocket Marathon is going to be held in March 2017.

Chapter 3
Current Conditions and Future Deployment of Broadband Services on Kuchinoerabu-jima Island
Masato MASUYA

Ultra-high-speed broadband services are widely available in Japan. However, such service has not been deployed to all remote Japanese islands; thus, residents on such remote islands cannot benefit from broadband Internet. In this article, I report the current conditions of the telecommunication environment on Kuchinoerabu-jima Island and suggest methods for the deployment of an ultra-high-speed broadband environment.

1. Introduction
Kuchinoerabu-jima Island, which is a part of Yaku-shima Town, is one of the Osumi Islands belongs to Kagoshima Prefecture, Japan. The island is located approximately 12 kilometers west of Yaku-shima Island (30.443 degrees north latitude and 130.217 degrees east longitude). It is an active volcanic island with an area of 38 square kilometers (12 kilometers long by 5 kilometers wide). The highest elevation on the island is Mt. Furudake with a height of 657 meters above sea level. The island consists of a northwestern old volcanic body of Mt. Banyagamine and a southeastern active volcanic complex of Mt. Furudake, Mt. Shindake, and Mt. Noike. According to a nationwide census conducted in July 2016, there are 122 residents and 74 households on the island.

There is no direct public transportation to Kuchinoerabu-jima Island from Japan's mainland. The local government of Yaku-shima Town has provided a regular ferry service between Kuchinoerabu-jima Island and Yaku-shima Island. It is a round trip service that operates once a day, and it takes 100 minutes to sail between the two islands. It is not possible to take a day trip to and from Kuchinoerabu-jima Island using public transportation. The ferry is often canceled due to adverse weather conditions, such as typhoons or strong winter winds. Logistics costs are high, and people and goods are not easy to transport. The residents of Kuchinoerabu-jima Island face many logistical disadvantages.

One of the most active volcanoes in Japan is located on Kuchinoerabu-jima Island. Mt. Shindake erupted violently with pyroclastic flows at 9:59 on May 29, 2015. The local government promptly ordered all residents to evacuate the island. Then, the evacuation order was lifted on December 25, 2015, except for some districts. The order for all districts was lifted on October 25, 2016. The last volcanic activity with a small eruption occurred on June 18, 2015. Since then, no volcanic activities have been observed. However, people should remain alert to any signs of volcanic activity.

If high-speed broadband Internet access becomes available, the distribution of information would be comparable to that of the mainland. Broadband is also useful to obtain various information about natural disasters, such as volcanic activity. Broadband is essential to improve living standards, economic development, and administrative efficiency. With broadband connectivity, it would be possible to promote content industries that do not require logistical operations, offer tourist information, and sell special local products over the Internet. The Internet can narrow the cultural and educational gap by providing various educational opportunities through e-learning and by acquiring news, weather reports, and entertainment, such as music and movies.

Nevertheless, a broadband environment has not been implemented on Kuchinoerabu-jima Island. The following statements about the conditions of the broadband environment on the island are based on a field survey conducted in 2014 and 2015; however, to date, the conditions have not changed.

2. Broadband environment in Japan

According to the 2016 White Paper on Information and Communications in Japan (Ministry of Internal Affairs and Communications, Japan 2016), the number of Internet users was 100.46 million. The penetration rate among the general population was 83.0% at the end of 2015. The usage rate for the 13 to 59 age group exceeded 90%, and it exceeded 80% for families with annual income greater than 4 million yen. Over 70% of respondents across all age groups accessed the Internet at least once per day. The most common activity was "sending and receiving emails," followed by "using weather forecasts" and "map or transportation information services."

Ultra-high-speed broadband services are commonly used to access the Internet. Those services include Fiber to the Home (FTTH), cable TV Internet, Fixed Wireless Access (FWA), Broadband Wireless Access (BWA), and Long-Term Evolution (LTE), which is a 3.9G wireless communication standard. Besides FTTH and LTE services, services with download speeds of 30 Mbps or higher are defined as ultra-high-speed broadband services. Ultra-high-speed broadband services were available in 55.94 million households or 99.9% of all Japanese households at the end of March 2015. Broadband services were available for all of Japan's 55.95 million households, including FTTH, Digital Subscriber Line (DSL), cable TV Internet, FWA, satellite Internet, BWA, LTE, and 3.5G mobile phone services. Satellite Internet access, which is available anywhere in Japan, was included in the definition of broadband service; thus, all households are assumed to have broadband services. However, satellite Internet access is costly and too expensive for ordinary people.

Broadband and ultra-high-speed broadband services employ fixed-line communication and mobile communication services. Fixed-line communication services include FTTH, DSL, cable TV, and FWA, and mobile communication services include BWA, LTE, satellite access, and 3.5G mobile phones.

At the end of March 2016, the penetration rate of fixed-line ultra-high-speed broadband was 56.5% (37.81 million subscriptions) and the penetration rate of fixed-line broadband was 68.4%. The rate of fixed-line communication services has been increasing gradually. For FTTH and DSL services, DSL has continued to experience a net decrease while FTTH services have seen consistent net increases. Subscriptions to fixed-line communication services are based on households, whereas those for mobile communication services are based on individuals. Therefore, the penetration rate of such services can only be calculated for fixed-line communication services.

Subscriptions to mobile ultra-high-speed broadband services are increasing dramatically each year. At the end of March 2016, there were 87.39 million subscriptions for 3.9G (LTE) services (up 28.9% from last year) and 35.21 million subscriptions for BWA services (up 80.9% from last year). Mobile communication services are being used more frequently in Japan, primarily due to the widespread use of smartphones.

3. Current broadband conditions on Kuchinoerabu-jima Island

Here, I report the broadband conditions on Kuchinoerabu-jima Island as of 2014 and 2015, with focus on fixed-line and mobile services.

3.1. Fixed-line communication services

Since 1982 (NEGISHI 1997), subscriber telephone services have been provided by NTT West on Kuchinoerabu-jima Island because such services are mandatory for incumbent telecommunication companies. Using telephone voice services, narrowband Internet access is possible using a dial-up connection with an analog modem, (less than 56 kbps). In many places in Japan, telecommunication carriers offer DSL services that are used to transmit data over copper telephone cable lines. However, DSL services are not available on Kuchinoerabu-jima Island

Fig. 1. NTT West's Tashiro Wireless Linking Station.

Fig. 2. NTT West's Kuchinoerabu Telephone Switching Station.

because a DSL Access Multiplexer (DSLAM), which concentrates multiple DSL connections, facilities have not been installed at telephone exchanges. Furthermore, other types of fixed-line broadband services, including FTTH, cable TV, and FWA, have not been provided on the island. Until now, only dial-up Internet access has been available on Kuchinoerabu-jima Island.

There are no technical difficulties associated with providing ultra-high-speed broadband services using optical fiber networks. The most significant barrier to broadband deployment in less favored regions has been its very high cost. Broadband deployment on islands faces two difficulties from a cost perspective. One is the "last mile" problem, which refers to making the connection between a subscriber and the nearest Internet access point, such as a telephone switching station. In this problem, communication lines that connect sparse households and the installation of facilities to provide Internet access are quite costly and unprofitable for telecommunication carriers. The other difficulty is the cost of implementing underwater optical cable networks. Underwater optical cables are the best way to connect the island to the backbone network on the mainland; however, this is quite costly to construct and maintain.

On more remote islands, if a sufficient number of subscribers are expected, a private telecommunication carrier may construct an underwater optical network to provide broadband services. On several islands with relatively large populations, broadband services are provided by private telecommunication carriers. However, on small islands like Kuchinoerabu-jima Island, the profitability of broadband deployment is insufficient for commercial services. For local governments, the cost of broadband deployment on islands has been a critical problem, even if the Japanese government provides financial support. Therefore, ultra-high-speed broadband has not been deployed and is not expected in the future on such remote islands.

The telecommunication carrier has connected facilities for subscriber telephone services to the external communication network on Kuchinoerabu-jima Island using microwave wireless access lines. The wireless linking facility of NTT West is located near Tashiro district on the way to Yumugi from Honmura district. This facility is called NTT West's Tashiro Wireless Linking Station (Fig. 1). The station is connected by optical fiber to the telephone switching station in Honmura district, which is called NTT West's Kuchinoerabu Telephone Switching Station (Fig. 2). The former wireless linking station is at the top of Mt. Banyagamine (Fig. 3). The former wireless linking station is now the evacuation center for the residents of Kuchinoerabu-jima Island.

The microwave wireless line network is sequentially linked through Kamegaoka in Minamisatsuma City, Kuro-shima Island in Mishima Village, Io-jima Island in Mishima

Village, Kuchinoerabu-jima Island, and Yaku-shima Island. This microwave wireless line network is connected to the optical fiber network on the mainland at Kamegaoka and Yaku-shima Island. From Kuchinoerabu-jima Island, there are two redundant routes to the mainland network through Io-jima Island and Yaku-shima Island. The bandwidth of the wireless line network is limited to 6 Mbps. Therefore, high-speed broadband data transmission over 10 Mbps is not possible on Kuchinoerabu-jima Island, even though some leased-line services for businesses have been utilized.

Each telephone line to households on Kuchinoerabu-jima Island is wired from NTT West's Kuchinoerabu Telephone Switching Station. Integrated Services Digital Network (ISDN) services, which are often used for narrowband Internet access, are available on the island; however, a limited number of services is provided by NTT West, and there are very few subscribers on the island. The ISDN data transfer rate is up to 64 kbps and constant connection with NTT's FLET'S ISDN services is not available on the island because the facilities are not installed at NTT West's switching station.

Therefore, on Kuchinoerabu-jima Island, there is no constant connection to the Internet by fixed-lines.

If NTT West's "Digital Access 1500" leased-line service was utilized, the maximum transfer rate would be 1.5 Mbps. However, the connection speed is not equivalent to broadband, and the monthly fee for the service would be more than 500,000 yen. It is assumed that few would subscribe to the service if it were offered.

3.2. Mobile communication services on Kuchinoerabu-jima Island

There are seven districts on Kuchinoerabu-jima Island, including Honmura, Maeda, Mukaehama, Shinmura, Nemachi, Tashiro, and Yumugi. Most households and the branch office of Yaku-shima Town are located in Honmura district, which is where the ferry terminal is located. Maeda, Mukaehama, and Shinmura districts are relatively close to Honmura district. Yumugi district is the second largest district on the island and is located in the southeastern region. It takes 30 to 40 minutes to drive from Honmura to Yumugi districts. Tashiro and Nemachi districts are very small districts on the road from Honmura to Yumugi districts.

Subscriber telephone services are available in every district on Kuchinoerabu-jima Island because they are universal services in Japan.

Fig. 3. Evacuation center (former wireless linking station) at the top of Mt. Banyagamine.

Fig. 4. NTT docomo's Banyagamine Base Station.

Fig. 5. NTT docomo's booster station in Honmura district.

Fig. 6. NTT docomo's booster station in Yumugi district.

However, mobile phone services are not available in all areas on the island. The coverage area for mobile phone services is determined by the location of the wireless base station of the mobile telecommunication carriers. With the exception of Yumugi district, wireless communication between mobile phones and the wireless base station located off Kuchinoerabu-jima Island is blocked by a mountain. In Yumugi district, mobile phones are able to communicate with the wireless base station in Yaku-shima Island. Two mobile telecommunication carriers, i.e., NTT docomo and Softbank, cover Honmura district, including Maeda, Mukaehama, and Shinmura districts, by installing wireless base or booster stations in Honmura district. Tashiro and Nemachi districts are mobile dead zones, where mobile phones cannot communicate with wireless base stations.

NTT docomo has installed a wireless base station at the top of Mt. Banyagamine and wireless booster stations in Honmura and Yumugi districts. The wireless base station at Mt. Banyagamine is called NTT docomo's Banyagamine Base Station (Fig. 4). The mobile booster station is the mobile telecommunication carrier's facility that repeats and increases signals from the wireless base station. The booster station in Honmura district (Fig. 5) boosts the signal from NTT docomo's Banyagamine Base Station and the station in Yumugi district (Fig. 6) boosts the signal from NTT docomo's Nagata Base Station in Yaku-shima Island. I assume that NTT docomo's Banyagamine Base Station is connected to NTT docomo's backbone network by NTT West's digital leased-line service. As mentioned previously, the bandwidth of this service is limited to 1.5 Mbps. Thus, NTT docomo's Banyagamine Base Station can only provide FOMA service, which is NTT docomo's 3.5th generation mobile telecommunication service. In Honmura, Maeda, Mukaehama, and Shinmura districts, only FOMA services are offered directly by NTT docomo's Banyagamine Base Station and indirectly by the wireless booster station in Honmura district, which boosts the signal of the wireless base station. The wireless communication bandwidth of mobile terminals that connect directly and indirectly to NTT docomo's Banyagamine Base Station are limited to 1 Mbps. All mobile phones and terminals in Honmura district must share that bandwidth. If two terminals connect to the Internet, the connection speed of each terminal is halved. In fact, this tendency was observed in a field survey on Kuchinoerabu-jima Island. The wireless booster station in Yumugi district boosts NTT docomo's Nagata Base Station, which offers Xi (LTE) service. When I measured the connection speed in Yumugi district, the speed was 2 Mbps or more.

Softbank has installed a wireless base station near the Maeda district on the outskirts of Honmura district (Fig. 7). Only the 3.5th generation mobile telephone services are offered. Softbank's wireless base station is connected to Softbank's backbone network via satellite communication. Therefore, a data connection is nearly impossible in Honmura district; however, telephone communication service is available.

For Yumugi district, Softbank has no wireless base stations or booster stations, but the district is considered a service area for Softbank 4G LTE because mobile phones and mobile terminals can connect to the wireless base station in Yaku-shima Island.

Another mobile telecommunications carrier, au by KDDI, has not installed wireless base stations or wireless booster stations on Kuchinoerabu-jima Island. Therefore, the island is outside the au service area. In Yumugi district, au's LTE services are available through a connection with the wireless base station in Yaku-shima Island.

The current mobile communication conditions on Kuchinoerabu-jima Island are summarized by district in Table 1.

In addition, a satellite Internet connection is used at the Kanagadake Elementary-Junior High School in Honmura district. However, it has only been used in the school and details are unavailable.

4. Deployment of a broadband environment on Kuchinoerabu-jima Island

There are no insurmountable technical difficulties associated with deploying a fixed-line ultra-high-speed broadband environment in Japan, even on Kuchinoerabu-jima Island. All it requires is laying optical cables. However, it is costly to lay optical cables, especially on remote isolated islands. Therefore, on Kuchinoerabu-jima Island, it would be very expensive to deploy an ultra-high-speed broadband environment. This is also true for local governments, such as Yaku-shima Town. Therefore, in this section, I propose cost-effective deployment methods for a broadband environment on Kuchinoerabu-jima Island.

For a broadband environment on Kuchinoerabu-jima Island, two groups of communication lines must be considered, i.e., interlinking lines from Kuchinoerabu-jima Island to the mainland and access lines from the base station to each household. As mentioned previously, the only connection to the mainland is NTT West's microwave wireless link, which is insufficient for broadband services. Only copper telephone cables have been laid on the island; thus, there are no optical cables for ultra-

Fig. 7. Softbank's PLB Yaku-shima-Kuchinoerabu-jima Base Station.

Table 1. Current mobile communication conditions on Kuchinoerabu-jima Island.

District	NTT docomo	Softbank	au by KDDI
Honmura (including Maeda, Mukaehama, and Shinmura)	3.5G (FOMA) (<1Mbps)	3.5G (3G) (no data connections)	N/A
Yumugi	LTE (Xi)	LTE (4G LTE)	LTE (4G LTE)
Tashiro and Nemachi	N/A	N/A	N/A

high-speed broadband services.

4.1. Interlinking Kuchinoerabu-jima Island and the mainland

There are several communication methods to connect Kuchinoerabu-jima Island to the mainland. In the following, I describe underwater optical cable lines, wireless links, and satellite connections.

4.2. Underwater optical cable lines

Underwater optical cables are ideal for interconnection between Kuchinoerabu-jima Island and the mainland. Redundant trunk lines are advisable to mitigate accidents and failures. Several underwater optical cable routes are possible, such as the route that connects to Yaku-shima Island or the route to Io-jima Island, as well as a direct link to the mainland.

An ideal route is a direct link to the mainland that can eliminate interference from other traffic. When it connects to the mainland network at two points, such as Yamagawa in Ibusuki City and Makurazaki City, redundancy will be ensured both in the sea and the ground. However, it costs over several hundreds of million yen to lay approximately 300 kilometers of optical cable. On the other hand, the length of the underwater line route to Yaku-shima Island is 10 to 20 kilometers. This would cost several tens of million yen. Meanwhile, the cost of the route to Io-jima Island is between the cost of the route to the mainland and the route to Yaku-shima Island. The underwater optical lines to the mainland from Io-jima Island would be laid by Mishima Village with financial support from the Japanese government, and they would not be provided by telecommunication carriers. It would be difficult to utilize the route to Io-jima Island because it would require significant consideration from Mishima Village.

Thus, I suggest the route to Yaku-shima Island as the best route for the underwater optical cable line. On Kuchinoerabu-jima Island, Honmura and Yumugi districts are recommended as the linking point of the underwater cable network and the ground cable network. In this case, a ground cable network between Honmura and Yumugi districts would be required, but underwater redundant trunk cables would be more functional.

4.3. Wireless links

NTT West has installed microwave wireless linking facilities on Kuchinoerabu-jima Island to connect their facilities for subscriber telephone services to their backbone networks on the mainland via Io-jima Island and Yaku-shima Island. NTT West's wireless linking facilities offer subscriber telephone services and do not have sufficient bandwidth for broadband service. Reinforcement of NTT West's facilities or the installation of a new wireless linking facility would be required to provide broadband service on Kuchinoerabu-jima Island using wireless lines.

Even if the wireless linking facilities on Kuchinoerabu-jima Island were upgraded, broadband service would not necessarily be available unless other wireless linking facilities to the mainland were also upgraded. However, it would cost too much to upgrade all related facilities. Upgrading NTT West's facilities is unreasonable. The remaining method is the installation of new wireless linking facilities. Although the bandwidth of wireless lines is less than that of underwater optical cables, it can be deployed at less cost than underwater optical cables.

If new wireless linking facilities are installed on Kuchinoerabu-jima Island, the optimal location of the wireless base station would be NTT West's Tashiro Wireless Linking Station or NTT docomo's Banyagamine Base Station, which have line of sight to both Io-jima Island and Yaku-shima Island. The wireless communication distance between the island and Yaku-shima Island is 25 kilometers, and the distance to Io-jima Island is 35 kilometers. Shorter communication links with Yaku-shima Island are preferable for stable and high-speed communication.

Several types of wireless linking equipment could be used. Among them, wireless equipment that uses 2.4 GHz, 5 GHz, 18 GHz, or 80 GHz bands are leading candidates for wireless linking facilities on Kuchinoerabu-jima Island. However, with the exception of the 2.4 GHz band, wireless station licenses are required for such equipment. Licensed equipment can utilize its own frequency and has more output power compared to non-licensed equipment; thus, stable and high-speed communication could be realized by long-distance transmission by suppressing surrounding influences, such as other wireless traffic. Incidentally, we can ensure the wireless link's redundancy by trunk connections to wireless links using a combination of several types of equipment that use different frequency bands. For example, Toshima Village could use 5 GHz and 18 GHz band wireless equipment to connect the islands because the distance between the islands is approximately 20 kilometers. I suggest that a trunk connection of license-required wireless equipment is more suitable for a wireless link on Kuchinoerabu-jima Island. On the other hand, unlicensed 2.4 GHz band equipment is less costly and is easy to deploy. However, with 2.4 GHz band wireless equipment, the installation location must be considered carefully to eliminate the effects of interference from other wireless facilities or weather conditions. I have previously reported investigation results of the 47.5-kilometer 2.4 GHz band wireless links over the sea (Masuya *et al.* 2012).

Furthermore, it may be necessary to consider the connection line between the wireless base station and the linking stations of each residence in the district. Candidates for wireless base stations, i.e., NTT West's Tashiro Wireless Base Station and NTT docomo's Banyagamine Base Station, are too far from the residential district. A direct wireless link between the wireless base station and the district is difficult. This seems to be why NTT docomo has installed the wireless booster station in Honmura district.

4.4. Satellite connection

A satellite connection is available to link Kuchinoerabu-jima Island to the mainland. Its bandwidth is limited to narrowband; thus, it is difficult to share a connection with several households. Therefore, satellite connection facilities would be necessary for each household. Access lines are not necessary for a satellite connection, and this is the only benefit of satellite connections. I do not recommend a satellite connection because it only realizes broadband connection to the Internet for individual households rather than the whole district, and it is not ultra-high-speed broadband.

4.5. Access lines on Kuchinoerabu-jima Island

To provide broadband service, access lines from a base station to each household are required in addition to linking the island and the mainland. In the following, I describe two types of wired methods, i.e., FTTH and DSL, and two types of wireless methods, i.e., LTE and Wi-Fi.

4.5.1. FTTH

The ideal method for access lines is FTTH. In this method, optical fiber would be laid to each residence from the linking station, which connects to the interconnection lines off the island. The FTTH architecture is classified into two categories, i.e., "single star" and "double star." The single star architecture is a point-to-point topology, and the double star architecture is a point-to-multipoint topology. In the double star architecture, there is an optical splitter between a central facility and each subscriber. The cost of both architectures is nearly the same. Optical fiber should be installed underground to avoid damage from natural disasters, such as typhoons and volcanic eruptions. Copper telephone lines have been laid underground on several Osumi islands.

4.5.2. DSL

DSL, which is a broadband Internet access service that uses existing telephone lines, can be provided by installing a DSLAM at a telephone switching station. This is relatively inexpensive because new cable lines are not required. However, DSL service is not ultra-high-speed broadband.

With ADSL, the longest line distance from the location of the DSLAM is 4 kilometers due to signal attenuation. If the DSLAM facility is installed at NTT West's Kuchinoerabu Switching Station, only Honmura district (including Maeda, Mukaehama, and Shinmura districts) would be covered by ADSL. Tashiro district may be covered; however, Nemachi and Yumugi districts would not be covered. In Yumugi district, ADSL service would not be necessary because LTE services are already available.

4.5.3. LTE

Yumugi district is already covered by LTE service areas through NTT docomo, au, and Softbank. We must consider how to cover other districts, especially the most populated Honmura district. The simplest solution is to upgrade the current NTT docomo wireless facility to LTE. To achieve that, both NTT docomo's deployment of LTE facilities to the Banyagamine base station and an ultra-high-speed broadband connection at the base station would be required. If the local government deploys an ultra-high-speed broadband interconnection, mobile telecommunication carriers may install new LTE capable facilities. For Tashiro and Nemachi districts, the installation of wireless booster stations is valid.

4.5.4. Wi-Fi

Wi-Fi is a technology for wireless access to the Internet. Wi-Fi provides services in public spaces via hotspots set up as either free-of-charge or commercial services, as well as in private homes and businesses. Wi-Fi is useful in evacuation centers for natural disasters. Public Wi-Fi stations are widespread throughout Japan. However, there is no Wi-Fi hotspot in public spaces on Kuchinoerabu-jima Island because no broadband environment has been deployed. Once broadband services become available, public Wi-Fi could be implemented on the island.

Until broadband is deployed, it may be possible to install public Wi-Fi using LTE in Yumugi district. In Honmura district, a satellite Internet connection may be used for Wi-Fi hotspots. In both districts, the bandwidth of the Internet access lines is inadequate; thus, personal computers, tablets, and smartphones cannot connect simultaneously over Wi-Fi. To install public Wi-Fi hotspot facilities on the island, an ultra-high-speed broadband environment is essential.

4.6. Practical method for deployment of a broadband environment on Kuchinoerabu-jima Island

The ideal method to deploy an ultra-high-speed broadband environment on Kuchinoerabu-jima Island is to employ underwater optical cables to connect the island and the mainland and to lay optical fiber to each household from the base station. However, telecommunication carriers are unlikely to accept the cost of laying optical fiber for such a small population.

Subscriptions to mobile communication services have been growing steadily in Japan. Providing LTE mobile communication services is the most urgent issue on Kuchinoerabu-jima Island. Ultra-high-speed mobile communication services must be implemented as soon as possible. To provide LTE services on the island, the bandwidth of the upper link of NTT docomo's Banyagamine Base Station must be increased. Underwater optical lines are preferable for expanding bandwidth, followed by the construction of microwave wireless access lines.

I suggest that national and local governments assume the cost of implementing interlinking lines between Kuchinoerabu-jima Island and the mainland or Yaku-shima Island. Then, the local government should ask mobile telecommunication carriers to offer LTE services. Financial support from various levels of government may be expected in some cases.

5. Conclusion

There are various disadvantages on Kuchinoerabu-jima Island because it is a small remote isolated island. Its geographical disadvantages are difficult to overcome. The Internet can reduce such geographical disadvantages; however, a broadband environment has not been deployed on the island. The telecommunication environment on the island is 20 years behind that of the mainland. The residents have not obtained the various benefits of broadband Internet access, including information about natural disasters, such as volcanic activities.

In this article, I have reported the current conditions of the telecommunication environment on Kuchinoerabu-jima Island and suggested practical methods for the deployment of an ultra-high-speed broadband environment. Considering the widespread use of smartphones in Japan, the best and easiest method for an ultra-high-speed broadband environment is LTE mobile communication services provided by mobile telecommunication carriers. Telecommunication carriers, as well as national and local governments, are expected to play important roles in the deployment of an ultra-high-speed broadband environment on Kuchinoerabu-jima Island.

References

NEGISHI, I. 1997. *Minami no shima ni ikanai ka–ritou no naka no ritou Kuchinoerabu-jima* (Let's go to the southern island–Kuchinoerabu-jima, the most isolated isolate island). 139 pp., Minami Nippon Shimbun Kaihatsu Center, Kagoshima. (in Japanese)

MASUYA, M., AOKI, K. and SHIMOZONO, K. 2012. Radio propagation characteristics of the longest-distance oversea wireless LAN system in Japan. Academic Information Processing Environment Research 15: 62–71. (in Japanese)

Ministry of Internal Affairs and Communications, Japan 2016. 2016 White Paper on Information and Communications in Japan. (in Japanese)

Chapter 4
Demographical Structure and Social Changes of the Villages in the Osumi Islands
– Reclamation, Migration, Extinction, Creation and Cultural Renaissance –

Shunsuke NAGASHIMA

1. Introduction

The villages in the Osumi Islands are demographically very interesting because of their diversity. Yaku-shima's depopulation stopped after it was registered as UNESCO World Heritage Site in 1993. The villages on the island are not burdened because the main road circles around the island and reaches to the furthest villages. This is also helped by the island's relatively small size and the key industries on the island do not call for conventional commuters. One village on the mountain that was revitalized acts as the cultural renaissance center for neo-civilization and nature preservation.

Tanega-shima has been welcoming migrants since the Meiji Era and has received 600 families from Koshiki-shima; they have suffered from disasters like many islands in Kagoshima and mainland Kyusyu. A quarter of Sakurajima's population was welcomed after the Big Volcanic Eruption of the Taisho Era. We introduce their culture as being revitalized from their native islands, like Toshidon, which is registered as UNESCO Intangible World Cultural Heritage.

Kuchinoerabu-jima experienced depopulation after the big volcanic eruption and changes in industrial structures. However, islanders have enlivened youth activities and a local museum with support from the outside. Mage-shima was a fishery village; however, all land is now occupied by a private company, which has an airstrip for military use, and is intending on profiting from big projects. Statistically it is considered an uninhabited island, but recently it has started having resident registrations.

2. Island population movement and diversity within the regions

It is rare to find cases that grasp three-dimensional regional population movement (third dimension being time) to a two-dimensional distribution; these cases are extreme and varied. Each island and village owns distinct space which is characterized by unique history, geography, migration policy, cultural inheritance, cultural creation etc.

3. Yaku-shima

Like other remote islands in Japan, there has been a prominent tendency toward long term depopulation through people perusing higher education and seeking employment. The forest service station withdraw from Kosugidani has resulted in it becoming a deserted village. The Shirakoyama area, a mountainous village in Isso Port, experienced a population decrease after the withdraw of the forest service station; however, some newcomers have come to settle since. It became a deserted village after the river overflowed resulting in an avalanche of sand

Fig. 1. The preserved study of late Sansei Yamao, a poet and ideologist, at Yaku-shima Shirakoyama.

and stones, but hippy-like people settled and have formed a base for cultural dispatch and environmental action. They have been involved in the success of forest protection activities (Figs 1–2).

In 1993, Yaku-shima became registered as UNESCO Natural World Heritage Site. Since then the island has had I-turners (people running lodgings, guides, nature lovers, intellectuals), U-turners seeking new business opportunities (lodgings, guides, and souvenir shops), people working in the tourism industry, distance learning schooling opportunities, etc. This has stabilized the island and this has continued for almost 20 years. The island has a large circular road that goes near the perimeter of the island, and the area between the mountains and the coast is not squeezed, and there hasn't been a phenomenon of seeing a decline in specific villages or areas. The first generation of I-turners are putting their effort into the islanders' education by being tour guides, and this is helping the population decline cease. These can also be seen throughout the country, although it is rare. The population decline of the central commercial area, southern and northern edge areas near the western part of the forest road of UNESCO site, and the population increase of the southern and eastern parts contradict with the naturalist tendency of societal formation.

4. Kuchinoerabu-jima

It is a special island- it was a British and Satsuma illegal trading base for approximately half a year around the late Edo period. It also became a border trading base hidden away from economic surveillance, trading with Kuchinoshima, an island lying on the south, for several years until 1952 when the US occupation ceased and it reversed to Japan. It is a sulphur production site and an area where people settled after the Meiji period and after WWII.

The island population was stable, having nearly 20 villages and reaching over 1500 residents. It produces white turmeric (*Curcuma zedoaria*), and there has been growing dissatisfaction with the disparities between different areas of Yaku-shima Island, and at one point have seen villages separate. With the decline of the sulphur industry and facing volcanic eruptions (Fig. 3), this has triggered an accelerated population decline and it is currently at 10% of what it used to be. This has almost restricted the residential areas to two. Islanders are planning to retain the elementary and middle schools by internal students operating on Hyotan Island (it is an island shaped like a calabash, hyotan, and is named after the famous children's puppet show on national television). The school for the elderly has a folk museum, and this has become a stable facility and is functioning as a regional social educational centre.

Youth promotion associations and elderly groups supporting the youth are starting to develop (this is the opposite of villages where the elderly proportionately occupy most of the population; those types are capable of becoming annihilated). A special regional promotion activity is in progress with an honorary university professor residing in the area and involving external university staff. In 2007, the island itself became a national park, and the Kuchinoerabu

Fig. 2. Mr.T, an intellectual leader and an environmentalist, has been living in a zero emission, carbon neutral way for 30 years , at Yaku-shima Shirakoyama.

Fig. 3. Kuchinoerabu-jima saw a rapid decline in population due to the volcanic activities. The older generation are starting to proactively accept and encourage people expressing individualities in the hope of bringing younger generation to/back to the island.

Guide Association is working toward a new guide system to showcase former villages, history, volcanos, village life, etc.

5. Mage-shima

This island has experienced one of the most unfortunate population changes in Japan. Residents of Ikeda, Sunosaki, Amadomari on Tanega-shima have had special fishing rights on Mage-shima from 1763, and they have occupied the area seasonally. They had cattle farms of the decedents of samurai in early the Meiji period, who had moved to the island, government-operated sheep farms in 1881, 80 households settled after WWII, a sugar factory, and the migration of dairy farmers from Hokkaido. Plantation damage caused by deer, droughts, wind, fire caused by lightening, and last year's cricket infestation is continuing to cause the population to decline (currently 358).

In 1979, a private development company started acquiring sites and in 1980 the island became an uninhabited island. In 2008 the population was registered as 6 people, and in 2009 4 people, 2010 4 people, 2011 3 men, and it has now gained the inhabited island status. In 2005 a national survey of the population was 15 people out of which 1 was a woman, and

Fig. 4. Centenary memorial commemorating Koshiki-shima residents migrating to Tanega-shima Noginohira village. There are 7 Koshiki-shima memorials like this in 7 villages.

all were construction employees. In the 2010 national census, there was a total of 11 men (10 in construction, 1 in manufacturing, all in secondary sector of the economy, all over 40, and they didn't own arable land). From July 2014 there have been no employees registered as residents. However it is treated as a Habited Remote Island as defined by the Ministry of Land, Infrastructure, Transportation and Tourism.

6. Tanega-shima

Even with the large-scale merger of municipalities in the Heisei era, it is the only island with multiple municipalities in Kumagegun. The island has an uneven distribution of wealth.

On the southern part of the island: Minamitane town, the National Space Development Agency of Japan occupies a base and has a demand for tourism and financially has more capacity. The north: Nishinoomote city is filled with tourists, and central areas: Nakatane town have agricultural farmlands and areas specializing in food industries. The island's population decline rate/change is diverse; they can be shown by municipalities (between the 2005 and 2010 censuses Nishinoomote dropped by 5.4%, Nakatane decreased by 6.8%, Minamitane decreased by 7.9%), villages, migrants from other areas of Japan (with the tendency for people of same/similar regions to merge), coastal and mountainous areas, industrial structures, etc.

Their history is deep and extremely interesting, which is deserving of a book, from the administration of clans, history of the pastures, history of migration acceptance, transition of the migrants, to the way their culture is inherited. Migrants were accepted during the Meiji and Taisho periods, and the population increased, but from middle of the Showa era (Showa 30s, from 1955) its population has been decreasing. In the Meiji era, 6 households moved from Yamakawa (mid-south region of the Kagoshima mainland), in Meiji 17 (1884), approximately 600 households moved from Koshiki-shima in Meiji 19-20 (1886-1887), 19 households from Bounotsu (southwest region of Kagoshima mainland), in Meiji 19 (1886), a few from Tokuno-shima in Meiji 28 (1895), and there was a group migration from Okinoerabu-

Fig. 5. The historical account, hung at the old community centre in Sakuraen.

Fig. 7. A stone temple, which stands in front of a memorial, and the sign 'Homeland of Toshidon' on the temple in Shimo-Koshiki-shima Teuchi village. Costume change of the Toshidon takes place there.

Fig. 6. The centenary memorial marking the migration of Sakurajima people, erected on Oct 2014. It is located near the airport, and this is 16th one.

Fig. 8. Toshidon items. The mask is a gift from Kagoshima University staff. The nose is sharp.

Fig. 9. The sign 'Homeland of Toshidon' at the community centre. The sign used to be by the road.

Fig. 10. Pictures and news articles of Toshidon at the community centre. The middle school student wasn't aware that Toshidon became UNESCO Intangible World Cultural Heritage. He hasn't been to Koshiki-shima.

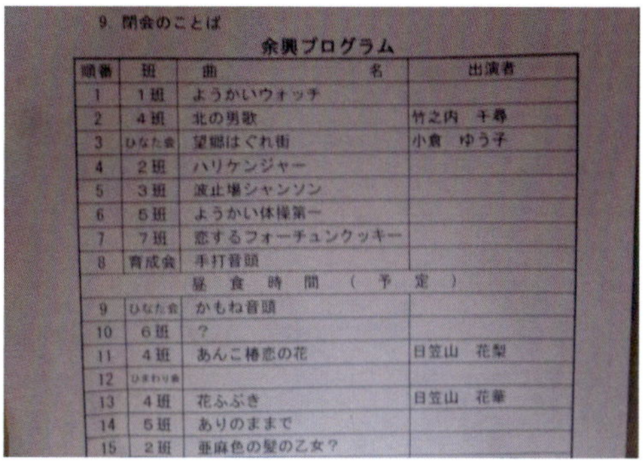

Fig. 11. Meeting to respect the elders in Teuchi. In the latter part of the morning musical performance took place.

Fig. 12. Toshidon making a sudden appearance on New Year's Eve at a house of a family originally from Kanagawa Prefecture in Kurazami village.

jima due to typhoons and droughts (Fig. 4). 10 households moved in from Kanagawa (Kanto region) in Meiji 30 (1897), and from Oita (northeastern Kyushu) and Shizuoka (Kanto region) too.

They have further received households from Kikai-jima, Amami-Oshima, Yoron-jima, Okinawa, Yamato mainland etc. And in year Taisho 3 (1914), 2,753 people (equivalent to 27% of former population) migrated from Sakurajima due to volcanic activity (Fig. 5), and in 2014 marked the centenary of the migration and have installed memorials to commemorate it (Fig. 6). Villages were sparsely formed in farm areas in the central mountainous area of Tenegashima where the main road runs from north to south.

Nishinoomote especially saw concentrated levels of migration during the beginning of Meiji era; out of 99 villages 30 saw migration. Migrants from Koshiki-shima has been said to die from starvation caused by typhoons but in reality, they have died from starvation caused by illnesses. From Meiji era, they had government fund supports and population increase was positively welcomed as part of the island's development. They also had the benefit of surplus of land. The tradition of Toshidon has been inherited and maintained in villages with migrants from Koshiki-shima. At the community centre in Noginohira (Figs 7–8), a banner saying 'Homeland of Toshidon' can be seen (Fig. 9). The adults and the children do not know about UNESCO Intangible Cultural Heritage appointments (Fig. 10). There is a will for an interaction with Koshiki-shima (Fig. 11), however people who have been rare. To commemorate the centenary, one of the villages enacted the revival of Toshidon. It is a village with migrants from Kagawa and Oita, but enthusiasm has been shown by people other than Shimo-Koshiki-shima residents at the end of 2014 (Fig. 12).

7. Concluding remarks

There are many records of the migration history of Tanega-shima, however there are not many comprehensive publications. The regional high school has its own 'local folk' club; it is deeply significant and interesting historically so one can expect for organizational and systematic preservation of the records.

Kuchinoerabu is an important research site for its disaster management history and has history which is characteristic of bordering remote islands. Local resources are becoming ready, and they need professional support. Mage-shima has been seeing rapid and over development, and now is in a crisis of retaining and preserving records of ecosystems, village history, educational history, industrial history, etc. It is essential to get public funding for this.

On Yaku-shima, migration research has been carried out to and from Kosugidani village by Kuwahara Research Group, Faculty of Law and Humanities of Kagoshima University. The quality of the Shirakawayama village historical records is not necessarily accurate even if they were kept amongst the residents there. Kamiyaku town (which was the northern administrative district on the island), unlike Yaku town (which was the southern administrative district on the island), lacks village journals recording the land's history, how one lived, its tradition, history, geography, etc. This requires urgent attention. The resources that are being collected are regionally maintained by the islands and are not public, and therefore there is scope for universities to collaborate and make them accessible to the wider public.

Chapter 5
Beginning of Food Production in the Osumi Archipelago

Hiroto TAKAMIYA and Naoko NAKAMURA

1. Introduction

The Osumi archipelago was occupied by *Homo sapiens* as early as 35, 000 years ago as evidenced from the Yokomine C and Tachikiri sites on the Tanega-shima island. Archaeological data from the archipelago have demonstrated that prehistoric culture in this region had been strongly influenced from the mainland southern Kyushu. For example, when Ishido (2014) reviewed the prehistory of this region, he noted close cultural similarities between southern Kyusyu mainland and the Osumi archipelago. He states that only time when the archipelago was independent from Kyushu was during the Late Yayoi period to the Kofun parallel preriods, when unique pottery culture emerged in the archipelago.

During the Yayoi period, food production, based mainly on rice, began in northwestern part of Kyushu and spread into most parts of the mainland Japan. What was happening in the Osumi islands during the Yayoi period? Did change in subsistence economy from hunting and gathering to food production also take place in the islands during the Yayoi period? Until 2015 we did not have any concrete evidence to demonstrate when food production began in the Osumi archipelago. In order to understand the beginning of food production in this region, this paper first review what we had known prior to 2015 in the mainland Kagoshima (and the Miyazaki prefecture, the other southern Kyushu region) and secondly in the Amami archipelago. This review would provide us some clues as to when the economic transition took place in the Osumi archipelago which is located between the mainland Kagoshima and the Amami archipelago. Thirdly, this paper will introduce the latest evidence on cultigens recovered from the Tanega-shima island and suggest when food production was likely accepted in this region.

2. Agriculture Origin in the mainland Kagoshima (and Miyazaki)

(see Table 1 for chronology, also see Fig. 1 for the locations of sites mentioned in the text)

The wet rice agriculture began in the northwest Kyushu during the Initial Yayoi (ca. 10th century BC). The Itatsuke site in Fukuoka city yielded one of the earliest evidence of rice agriculture in Japan. Then it spread to north and south. When did it arrive at Kagoshima? As early as 1962 and 1963, the archaeological excavation at the Takahashi shellmidden in Kimpo town unearthed Early Yayoi pottery, a polished stone sward, stone sickles and stone knives. All of which indicated that the wet rice agriculture reached to the western part of Kagoshima by the Early Yayoi period (Kawaguchi 2002: 38). Moreover in 1986, the Shimohara site, also located in Kimop town, yielded the Initial Yayoi pottery, stone knives and rice husks (Kawaguchi 2002: 38). The excavation revealed that the rice agriculture reached the area almost simultaneously as it appeared in Fukuoka.

However, a question arises from the above findings. That is, while one can speculate presence of rice agriculture based on these findings, it is difficult to determine whether or not it was wet or dry rice agriculture. Which one was it? The Kagoshima University Campus site at Korimoto Housing Complex shed light on this question. The layer which dated to ca. 2460±60 BP yielded not only actual paddy fields but also numerous footprints (Kawaguchi 2002: 39). This piece of evidence demonstrates that wet rice agriculture spread to this area by the Initial Yayoi period.

It should be mentioned that rice agriculture

also diffused into Miyazaki prefecture at about the same time. The Kurotsuchi site, the Hijiana site and the Sakamoto A site, all of which are located in Miyakonojo city, provided archaeological data on rice agriculture. The Kurotsuchi site yielded stone knives, rice tempered pottery sherd, and large amount of rice phytolith (KUWAHATA and YOKOYAMA 2000: 7, KAWAGUCHI 2002: 39, NAKAMURA et al. 2013: 17). Interestingly, Fujiwara (in KUWAHATA and YOKOYAMA 2000: 7) who examined rice phytolith from the site thinks the rice cultivated at or near the site was dry field rice agriculture. The Hijiana site also unearthed stone knives, chipped stone axes probably used for digging and large amount of rice phytolith (KUWAHATA and YOKOYAMA 2000: 7). KUWAHATA and YOKOYAMA (2000) feel wet rice agriculture was practiced at or near the site. These two sites also yielded Paniceae and suggesting foxtail millet, broomcorn millet and/or barnyard millet might have been cultivated. Finally, the wet rice paddy field was recovered from the Sakamoto A site. These pieces of evidence demonstrate that both wet and dry rice agriculture was practiced in Miyakonojo city during the Initial Yayoi period.

Recently, NAKAMURA et al. (2013) have conducted pottery impression analysis from the Kurotsuchi site and the Sakamoto B site, which is located near the Sakamoto A site. From the former, they have identified foxtail millet, foxtail millet or green foxtail, rice, shiso (Perilla sp.) and unknown species. NAKAMURA et al. (2013: 17) agree with FUJIWARA's remark on dry rice agriculture being practiced at or near the site. From the Sakamoto B site they have identified rice and possible foxtail millet (2013: 16). Based on the study, NAKAMURA et al. (2013: 17) conclude that rice and foxtail millet were cultivated during the Initial Yayoi in Miyazaki. They also suggest that foxtail millet

Table 1. Chronology of mainland Japan, Amami, and Osumi archipelagos.

B.P.	Mainland Japan (except Hokkaido)		Amami		Osumi Archipelago
ca.11/12~15 AD	Historic	Kamakura to Muromachi	Gusuku		Kamakura to Muromachi
		Asuka to Heian		Late 2	Asuka to Heian
1400					
1700	Kofun	Kofun		Late 1	Kofun parallel
2400-2900	Yayoi	Yayoi			Yayoi
3200	Jomon	Final Jomon	Shell Midden	Early 5	Final Jomon
4500		Late Jomon		Early 4	Late Jomon
5500-6000		Middle Jomon		Early 3	Middle Jomon
6000		Early Jomon		Early 2	Early Jomon
7500-8000				Early 1	
11000-12000		Initial Jomon		Biginning of pottery culture?	Initial Jomon
16000	Incipient Jomon		Palaeolithic		Incipient Jomon
35000	Paleolithic				Paleolithic

Note: The mainland chronology is provided as a rough guide.
Periodization between the Amami archipelago and mainland Japan does not always corresponded exactly.

The Osumi Islands

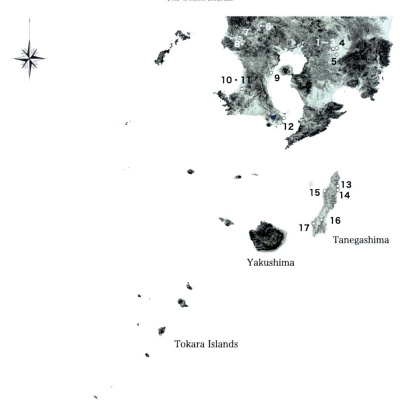

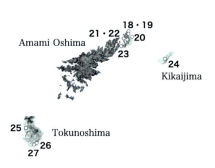

1	Sakamoto A・B	8	Kusumoto	15	Kamiyokino	22	Sauchi
2	Hoshihara	9	Kagoshima University Campus	16	Tachikiri	23	Hango
3	Tsuruhami	10	Shimohara	17	Yokomine C	24	Gusuku site group
4	Hijiana	11	Takahashi	18	Yomisaki	25	Nakagumi
5	Kurotsuchi	12	Hashimuregawa	19	Arago	26	Kawaminetsuji
6	Suitenmukai	13	Shimohagimine	20	Matsunoto	27	Omonawa 1・4
7	Kyoden	14	Izumibaru	21	Akakina Gusuku	28	Sumiyoshi

Fig. 1. The locations of sites mentioned in the text.

might have been cultivated during the early Final Jomon.

Thus during the Initial Yayoi period, both wet and dry rice agriculture appeared to have been practiced in Kagoshima and Miyazaki prefectures. In addition, millets were likely cultivated. While archaeological data have not been accumulated enough, available data suggest food production was practiced during the following periods. In Miyazaki, for example, at the Sakamoto A site, rice paddy fields have been identified at the late Early Yayoi period, late Middle Yayoi period, Final Yayoi period, and the Medieval period layers (KAWAGUCHI 2002: 42). Nakamura et al. have identified rice impression from the Early Yayoi period pottery and the Middle Yayoi period pottery at the Sakamoto B site (NAKAMURA et al. 2013: 16). Also foxtail millet impressions from the Early and Middle Yayoi pottery recovered from the Kurotsuchi site (NAKAMURA et al. 2013: 16). They have reported foxtail millet and broomcorn millet impressions from the late Late to Final Yayoi pottery sherds from the Hoshihara site. The site also yielded rice, broomcorn millet and foxtail millet impressions from the Middle Kofun period pottery as well as pottery sherds dating to the 9th to 10th centuries AD. A rice impressed pottery sherd is reported from the Tsuruhami site, dating to the Late Kofun period.

In Kagoshima prefecture, the Kagoshima University Campus site at Korimoto Housing Complex yielded wet rice paddy fields dating to the Middle Yayoi period (ONISHI et al. 2012: 99). The Kyoden site, the Middle Yayoi period, in Sendai city unearthed wet rice paddy fields and numerous rice phytolith. The Kusumoto site, located near the Kyoden site and dates to the Final Yayoi period also yielded numerous rice phytolith. Furthermore, both the Kyoden and Kusumoto sites unearthed various wooden tools which were used for agriculture, such as wooden hoes (KAWAGUCHI 2002: 40–41). According to HONDA (in KAWAGUCHI 2002:43), stone knives tend to increase during the Late Yayoi period in southern Kyushu, suggesting (rice) agriculture had become more important subsistence economy towards the end of the Yayoi period.

As to the Kofun period, the Kagoshima University Campus site at Korimoto Housing Complex yielded large amount of rice phytolith. Rice grains were recovered at SK 71 at the site as well (ONISHI et al. 2012:99, SHIMOYAMA 1995: 184). At the Hashimuregawa site in Ibusuki city unearthed hoe marks and Paniceae and rice phytolith. At the site, archaeologists have recovered ridge marks dating to the Heian period. The Mizumoto site, dating to the Medieval to the early Modern period, yielded rice, wheat, and possible millets. Thus in the southern Kyushu area, agriculture began at the beginning of the Yayoi period and continuously practiced since then. Now let us examine the situation in the Amami archipelago.

3. The Amami archipelago

Before we discuss about the beginning of food production in the archipelago, the chronology of this region should be introduced since the archipelago has different chronological scheme from the mainland Japan (Table 1). The prehistoric period in the archipelago consists of the Paleolithic, the Shellmidden and the Gusuku period. The Shellmidden period is further subdivided into the Early and Late periods. The Early period consists of Early 1 to 5 and the Late period of Late 1 and Late 2. Approximate dates are indicated in Table 1. When food production was introduced into this region?

During the 1980s, discovery of Yayoi pottery from the Sauchi site suggested that rice agriculture diffused into Amami during this period (KAWAGUCHI 1978). However, since no cultigens or agriculture related features had been unearthed from the Amami islands, this suggestion had been inconclusive.

In 1997, flotation was applied for the first time in this region at the Yomisaki site, dating to the 5th century AD (TAKAMIYA and CHIDA 2014). All plant remains obtained from the site belonged to wild species such as nuts. While only small amount of plant remains were recovered from the site, the result strongly implied that Yayoi agriculture did not diffuse to the Sauchi site or to the archipelago. Since 1997, flotation has been applied in many archaeological sites on the Amami islands. The following sites belong to the Shellmidden period: the Hango (Early 2, Takamiya in press a), the Arago (middle Late, Takamiya and Chida 2014), the Matsunoto (middle to late Late, Takamiya and Chida 2014) on Amami Oshima island, the Omonawa No. 1 (middle Late, Takamiya 2016), the Tobaru site (Early 5, Takamiya in press b) and Omonawa No.4 (Early 3 to Early 4, Takamiya 2016) on Tokuno-shima island, and the Sumiyoshi Shellmidden (Early 5, Takamiya and Chida 2014) on Okinoerabu island. While plant remains recovered from the above sites were small, all sites yielded wild species such as nuts and wild kiwi. The result strongly indicates the Shellmidden people were gatherers of the wild plants.

In 2002, Takamiya (in Takamiya and Chida 2014) had an opportunity to analyze plant remains recovered from flotation at the Akakina Gusuku. Based on artifacts recovered from the site, it was dated to 12th to 13th centuries AD. The result was astonishing. While only 6 litters of soil samples were processed by flotation, more than 200 plant remains were recovered. Interestingly, approximately 180 of these were rice. Other plant remains were barley and millets. The analysis demonstrated for the first time that the subsistence economy during the Gusuku period in this region was agriculture.

Between 2006 and 2016, several late Shellmidden and initial Gusuku period sites were excavated and soil samples for flotation were collected . These sites are the Gusuku site group on the Kikai-jima island (Takamiya and Chida 2014), the Kawaminetsuji site (Takamiya 2010) and the Nakagumi site (Takamiya and Chida 2013) on the Tokuno-shima island. The Gusuku site group consists of eight sites and soil samples were collected from seven of these sites. All these sites yielded cultigens such as barley, wheat, foxtail millet and broomcorn millet. The result suggests that food production was the major subsistence economy by this time period in the Amami archipelago. Furthermore, three rice grains from the Akakina Gusuku were carbon 14 dated. The dates of these were between the 11th to 12th centuries AD. In addition, nine cultigens (rice, burley, wheat, and foxtail millet) from the Gusuku site group (three sites) were also carbon 14 dated. They belonged to between the 8th to 11th centuries AD. Thus food production began somewhere between the 8th and 11th centuries AD in the Amami archipelago.

These reviews from Kagoshima (and Miyazaki) and the Amami archiplegao suggest that food production began in the Osumi archipelago somewhere between as early as the Initial Yayoi period and at the latest by the 8th to 11th centuries AD.

4. The Beginning of food production on the Osumi Archipelago

Torao (2006 in Nakamura 2015) and Nakamura (2006 in Nakamura 2015) based on written documents write that by the late 7th century AD, rice agriculture was practiced in this region. Archaeologists seem to have different view. Ishido (2014) has analyzed stone tools recovered from the Tanega-shima Islands and noticed that during the Jomon period, grind stones and stone dishes preoccupy among stone tool assemblages. He interprets that these stone tools were used for processing nuts. During the Yayoi to the Kofun parallel period, these two types of stone tools decrease in the stone tool assemblage. He argues this change in stone tool assemblage indicate that rice agriculture was introduced to the islands.

Then he reviewed available archaeological and other related data on subsistence economy during the Yayoi and Kofun parallel periods. His report implies agriculture (rice or millets) might have been practiced during the periods in concern. For example, in 1955, Kokubu and Morizono (Kokubu and Morizono 1955 in Ishido 2014) reported rice impressed pottery sherd dating to the Kofun parallel period. Also since 2000, some sites yielded agriculture related features, rice impressed pottery sherds and agriculture related tools. However, all of these findings are indecisive. Some pottery sherds were found with rice impressions but were not precisely dated. Some stone tools look like stone knives but were difficult to provide final decisions because of their morphologies were not exactly ones used in the mainland Japan.

After all, three pieces of information provides presence of agriculture in the Tanega-shima island during the Yayoi to the Kofun parallel periods (ISHIDO 2014). Firstly, isotopic values from human bones from the Hirota site (Yayoi site) were similar to those of rice agriculturists in Kyushu. Secondly, the stone tool assemblages indicate that during the Yayoi to Kofun parallel periods they are different from the Jomon, which suggests subsistence economy was different from the Jomon. Thirdly, some pottery sherds, which belong to the periods in concern bore rice impressions. Accordingly, ISHIDO (2014) feels that agriculture was practiced on the Tanega-shima island during the Yayoi to Kofun parallel periods. HASHIMOTO (2012: 22) believes that since Yayoi pottery diffused to Tanega-shima island, agriculture was likely diffused there. However, he also suggests that people on the island quit farming and became hunter-gatherers again during the Kofun period since only little influence can be detected from the mainland Kofun culture to Tanega-shima island.

Since not much archaeological excavations have been conducted on the other islands in the archipelago, it is not yet understood when food production was introduced. Based on study on the stone assemblages, ISHIDO (2014) finds that the stone tool assemblage in the Yaku-shima island was mostly preoccupied by the grinding stones and stone dishes. Since these types of stone tools were frequently recovered from the Jomon site, he suggests that the Yaku-shima island was occupied by hunter-gatherers at least until the Kofun parallel period.

While ISHIDO (2014) has reviewed intensively all available archaeological and written data, as of 2014, no hard evidence such as rice grains and/or rice paddy field had been known in this region. Thus it was not possible to suggest exactly when food production was introduced into the Osumi archipelago.

In 2015, NAKAMURA (2015) conducted pottery sherd impression analysis. She has analyzed pottery sherds recovered from the Izumibaru site, Shimohagimine site, and Kamiyokino site,

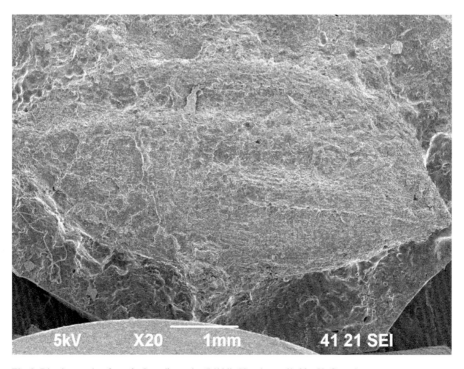

Fig. 2. Rice impression from the Izumibaru site (Middle Yayoi; supplied by H. OBATA).

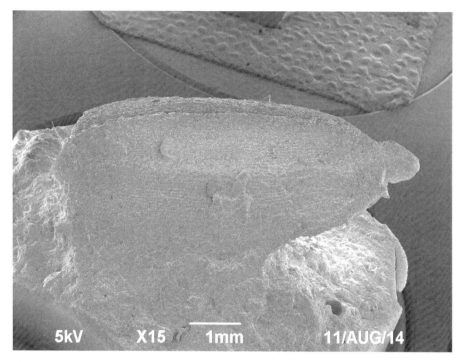

Fig. 3. Rice impression from the Shimohagimie site (Middle Yayoi; supplied by H. Obata).

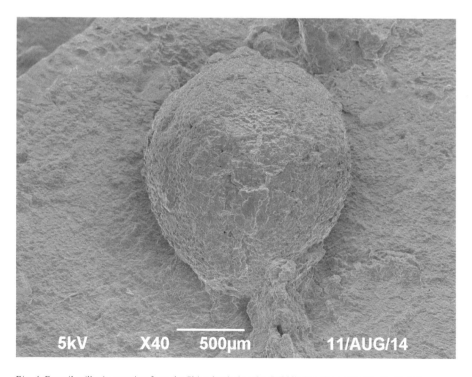

Fig. 4. Foxtail millet impression from the Shimohagimine site (Middle Yayoi; supplied by H. Obata).

locating northern part of the island. She analyzed 1,098 pieces, 1,080 pieces and 3,444 pieces of pottery sherds respectively. The Izumibaru site date mainly to the Middle Yayoi period. From the site, she has successfully identified 8 pottery sherds with impressions. Two of them were rice impressions (Fig. 2). Four of them were unknown seeds, one with a wood chip and the other with possible leaf fragment. The Shimohagimine site dates to the Middle Yayoi. Three pottery sherds with impression were recognized. One was with rice (Fig. 3), the other was with foxtail millet (Fig. 4), and the third one with possible beetle. The Kamiyokino site is dated to Middle Yayoi and the late Kofun period. Three pottery sherds, dating to the late Kofun period, exhibit plant impressions. Two of them were rice (Fig. 5) and the third one was unknown one. They date to the late Kofun period. According to NAKAMURA (2015), among these sherds, only one piece was introduced from Kyushu and other pottery sherds were locally manufactured.

The analysis demonstrates that people on the island knew rice and foxtail millet by the Middle Yayoi to Kofun parallel period. The question would be whether rice and foxtail millet were cultivated on the island or imported from (probably) Kyushu. While NAKAMURA (2015) considers possibility of the result of exchange, because rice was more or less constantly recovered from the Middle Yayoi to Kofun parallel period on pottery sherd analysis, she hypothesizes that agriculture was practiced on the island.

The following pieces of information might support Nakamura's hypothesis. As mentioned above carbon and nitrogen analysis of human bones from the Hirota site indicated the possibility of consumption of agricultural products (ISHIDO 2014). Secondly, so-called shoe shape axe was recovered from the Shimohagimine site. MITOMO et al. (1953 in NAKAMURA 2015) felt that the shoe shape axe was used as digging tool for dry field rice agriculture. Two other sites, the Atake cave site and the Izumibaru site, also yielded the shoe shape axe, dating to the Middle Yayoi period.

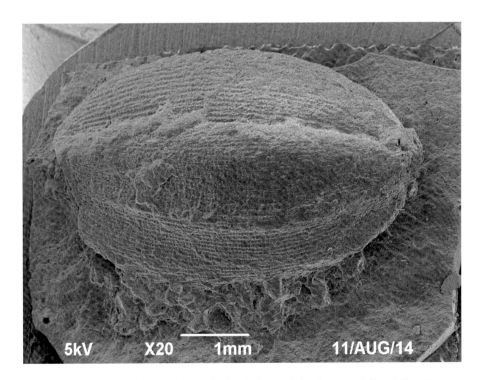

Fig. 5. Rice impression from the Kamiyokino site (late Kofun parallel or later; supplied by H. OBATA).

Also, as mentioned in the Kagoshima section, agriculture was diffused into the mainland Kagoshima by the Initial Yayoi period, especially to the Osumi peninsula as well. The distance between the Osumi peninsula and Tanega-shima island is about 40 km. Thus it is possible that food production was accepted on Tanega-shima island as early as the Initial Yayoi period.

5. Summary and Conclusions

This paper examined when food production was introduced to the Osumi archipelago. In order to understand the agriculture origin in the Osumi archipelago, where data related to the theme are scarce, the paper summarized the agriculture beginnings in the Kagoshima mainland (and Miyazaki) and the Amami archipelago. In the former, agriculture based on rice and millets began as early as the Initial Yayoi period. While cultigens recovered from the mainland Kagoshima (and Miyazaki) are still in small in number, they indicate that food production continuously practiced there from the Initial Yayoi to the historic period. On the other hand, on Amami islands, no cultigens were reported from the Shellmidden period. This indicates the hypothesis that food production (including rice agriculture) was introduced from Taiwan or southern China via the Ryukyu archipelago must be rejected. On the other hand, recent studies demonstrate that the earliest evidence of cultigens come from the 8th to 11th centuries AD sites. Therefore, it was speculated that agriculture in the Osumi archipelago began sometime between the Initial Yayoi and the 8th to 11th centuries AD.

In the Osumi archipelago, there was not enough hard data (plant remains, an agriculture field, for example) and agriculture beginning had not been well understood. ISHIDO (2014) has collected and studied all available data concerning agriculture beginning on Tanega-shima island and reached the conclusion that food production began there during the Yayoi period. This was also suggested by HASHIMOTO (2012) although he thought agriculture was abandoned during the Kofun parallel period.

NAKAMURA (2015) has provided an excellent data from pottery impression analysis. She analyzed the Middle Yayoi to the Kofun period pottery sherds and identified rice and foxtail millet impressions on five pottery sherds. The result indicated to her that rice agriculture was practiced during the above mentioned period. Other secondary data such as carbon and nitrogen analysis on human bones, so called shoe shape axes and close distance between mainland Kagoshima and the Osumi archipelago, might support her conclusion, which is also the conclusion reached by ISHIDO (2014).

Considering the short distance between the Osumi peninsula of the mainland Kagoshima and Tanega-shima island, agriculture might have started as early as the Initial Yayoi. Further pottery sherd impression analysis and actual excavation on Tanega-shima island will reveal when actually food production was introduced to the island. In addition to agriculture origin in Tanega-shima island, we need to examine what kind of cultigens were cultivate during the Yayoi period and the Kofun parallel period. Also in order to understand when subsistence change from hunting and gathering to agriculture took place in the Osumi archipelago as a whole, we need to conduct excavations on the other islands as well in the near future.

Acknowledgement

Professor Hiroki OBATA (Kumamoto University) has kindly provided photos used in this paper. We sincerely thank him for his kindness.

References

OHNISHI, T., MANABE, A., SANGAN, T., KANEGAE, K. and NAKAMURA, N. 2012. *Bisho-shoibutsu/bisho-konseki no bunsekini motozuku shokuyo shokubutsu no chosa-tokuni SLWdeno torikumi wo chushin ni* (A study on edible plants based on the analyses of micro plant remains and micro impressions). Kagoshima Koko 42: 99–108. (in Japanese)

HASHIMOTO, T. 2012. *Kofun Chikuzo Shuen Chiiki ni okeru Kyokaikeisei-Nangen shakai to Kokka keisei* (The formation of boundary in the peripheral regions during the Kofun building times-the southern boundary society and the state formation). Kokogaku Kenkyu 58(4): 17–31. (in Japanese)

ISHIDO, K. 2014. *Osumishoto no Senshi bunka ni mirareru Seigyo no Tokucho to Hensen* (The subsistence economy and its change in the prehistoric cultures in the Osumi archipelago). In: Takamiya, H. and Shinzato, T. (eds), *Ryukyu Retto Senshi/Genshi Jidai no Kankyo to Bunka no Hensen*, pp.159–170. Rokuichi Shobo, Tokyo. (in Japanese)

KAWAGUCHI, M. 2002. *Minami Kyushu ni okeru Inasaku bunka to Mokuseihin-saishin no chosa seika kara* (Rice agriculture and wooden tools in the southern Kyushu- from the latest excavation results). Gekkan Bunkazai 11: 38–43. (in Japanese)

KAWAGUCHI, T. 1978. *Sauchi Iseki* (The Sauchi Site). Kasari Town Board of Education, Kasari Town. (in Japanese)

KUWAHATA, M. and YOKOYAMA A. 2000. *Inasaku bunka ha minami Kyushu ni dou hiromattaka- Miyazaki Ken nairikubu no Isekikara* (How rice agriculture spread into the southern Kyushu-from inland sites in the Miyazaki prefecture). Rekishi Kyushu 11: 2–10. (in Japanese)

NAKAMURA, N. 2015. *Tanega-shima Doki Akkon Chosa kara mita Yayoi/Kofun Jidai Heikouki no Shokuyo Shokubutsu* (The food plants during the Yayoi and the Kofun Parallel periods as seen from Tanega-shima island pottery sherds impression analysis). (in Japanese)

NAKAMURA, N., MANABE, A., OHNISHI, T., SANGAN, T., FUKUI, T. and KUWAHATA, M. 2013 *Miyakonojo shi ni okeru Doki Akkon no Chosa-saibai shokubutsu no Donyu ni kanrenshite* (Pottery sherds impression analysis in Miyakonojo city-concerning the introduction of cultivated plants). Miyazaki Koko 24 (bottom): 15–29. (in Japanese)

SHIMOYAMA, S. 1995. *Koukogaku kara mita Hayato no Seikatsu-'Hayato' Mondai to Tembo* (The life ways of the Hayato as seen from archaeology-the questions and prospects on the Hayato). In: Shinkawa, T. (ed.), *Saikai to Nanto no Seikatsu/Bunka*, pp.169–199. Meicho Shuppan, Osaka. (in Japanese)

TAKAMIYA, H. 2010. *Kawaminetuji Iseki Shutsudo no Shokubutsu Itai* (The plant remains recovered from the Kawaminetsuji Site). In: Shinzato, A. (ed.), *Kamaminetsuji Iseki*, pp.77–79. Isen Town Board of Education, Isen Town. (in Japanese)

TAKAMIYA, H. 2016. *Omonawa Dai 1, Dai 4 Kaizuka shutsudo no Shokubutsu Itai* (The plant remains recovered from the Omonawa No.1 and No.4 sites). In: Shinzato, A. (ed.), *Omonawa Kaizuka Hakkutsu Hokokusho*, pp.140–141. Isen Twon Board of Education, Isen Town. (in Japanese)

TAKAMIYA, H. in press a. *Hango Iseki Shutsudo no Shokubutsu Itai* (The plant remains recovered from the Hango site). In The Collection of Papers for the memory of Dr. Kiyomi NAKAYAMA. (in Japanese)

TAKAMIYA, H. in Press b. *Tobaru Iseki Shutsudo no Shokubutsu Itai* (The plant remains recovered from the Tobaru site). In: Gushiken, R. (ed.), *Tobaru Iseki*. Amagi Town Board of Education, Amagi Town. (in Japanese)

TAKAMIYA, H. and CHIDA, H. 2013. *Nakagumi Isekikara Kenshutsu sareta Shokubutsu Itai* (The plant remains recovered from the Nakagumi Site). In: Gushiken, R. (ed.), *Nakagumi Iseki*, pp.46–48. Amagi Town Board of Education, Amagi Town. (in Japanese)

TAKAMIYA, H. and CHIDA, H. 2014. *Ryukyu Retto Senshi/Genshi Jidai niokeru Shokubutsu Riyo* (The plants use during the Pre-and Proto-historic times in the Ryukyu Archipelago). In: Takamiya, H. and Shinzato, T. (eds), *Ryukyu Retto Senshi/Genshi Jidai no Kankyo to Bunka no Hensen*, pp.127–142. Rokuichi Shobo, Tokyo. (in Japanese)

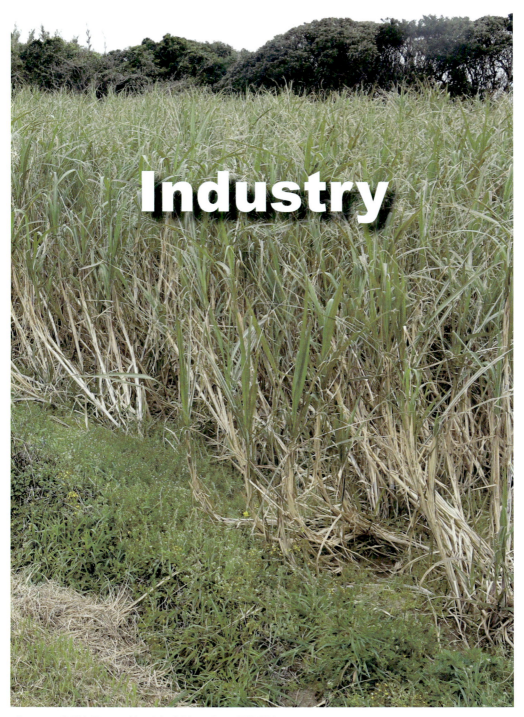

Industry

Sugarcane field in Tanega-shima Island. Photo: Ryuta TERADA

Chapter 6
Profile of Industries in Tanega-shima, Yaku-shima and Mishima-mura

Satoru NISHIMURA

1. Introduction

The paper briefly introduces the structure of industry in selected islands of Osumi Islands, or Tanega-shima, Yaku-shima and Islands in Mishima-mura with the use of basic statistics data provided by the municipal offices and others. After introducing the general features such as population, it describes the details of several industrial sectors which are important to the islands such as agriculture, manufacturing, service industry. It also introduces the contents of the paper in this chapter of "Industry in Osumi Islands" in the book.

2. Profiles of the industry in the islands

2.1. Tanega-shima Island

Tanega-shima Island is consisted of one city, or Nishinoomote and two towns, or Nakatane and Minamitane. Its population is 31,574 according to the results of the national census taken on Oct. 1, 2010.

The total production in the Island was 94.5 billion Yen in 2010 according to 'Census of Manufacturers, 2010'. The share of primary industry was 9.1 % compared to 1.4 % in Japan. Agriculture is more important in Tanega-shima Islands than other areas in Japan. The share of secondary industry is 11.6 % compared to 25.2 % in Japan. The average size of the establishments which had more than four employees was 14.3 in 2010. The main categories of the industries were related to food processing which shared 42.5 % of the total sale in 2010 as table 1 illustrates. The local products such as sugar and sweet potato are the materials for the industry. Sugar, schochu (clear liquor distilled from sweet potatoes) and starch are the products.

Besides agriculture and food processing industries, the island has other industrial resources. The examples are the industries based on the traditional culture such as 'Tanega-shima Scissors' and those based on the rocket launch base which is the biggest in Japan. The Japan Aerospace Exploration Agency (JAXA) is designated as a core performance agency to support the Japanese government's overall aerospace development. The base in the island is creating jobs and it also

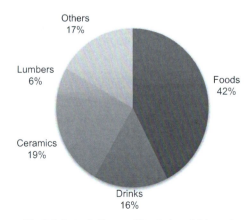

Fig. 1. Industry in Tanega-shima (value of shipment in 2010). Source: Nishiniomote Twon, Nakatane Town and Minamitane Town (2014).

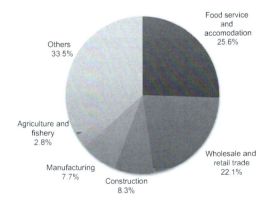

Fig. 2. Number of establishments in Yaku-shima (2014). Source: Yaku (2015).

contributes to the tourism industry especially when JAXA launches a rocket.

2.2. Yaku-shima Island

There is only one town in Yaku-shima Island which is Yaku. The population of the island was 13,589 according to the results of the national census taken on Oct. 1, 2010.

The share of primary industry based on the number of employees was 13 % compared to 1.4 % in Japan according Census of Manufacturers, 2010. Agriculture is more important in the island than other areas in Japan. Fruits production is the main activity in agriculture which consisted of 48.1 % of the all agricultural production in 2014. Several kinds of citrus such as ponkan (*Citrus reticulata*) and tankan (*Citrus tankan*) are produced there. The share of secondary industry was 15 % in 2010 compared to 25.2 % in Japan. The tertiary industry consisted 72 % of all the industry in 2010.

Tourism is one of the most important industries in the island. The island's ancient forest, which has been a natural World Heritage Site since 1993, attracts both domestic and overseas tourists. The number of food service and accommodation establishments was 286 which consisted of 25.8 % of all in 2010 as figure 2 shows. The data shows how import the tourist-related industries are in the island.

2.3. Mishima Village

Mishima village is consisted of three inhabited islands of Iō-jima, Kuro-shima and Take-shima and the uninhabited islands of Shōwa Iō-jima and Den-shima. As of December 2017, the village has an estimated population of 388.

The village produces Japanese black beef. Kuro-shima has more beef raising farmers than other two islands. Shitake mushroom and bamboo shoots are also produced. Iō-jima produces camellia oil which is also used for production of soap, shampoo and conditioner. These products gain wide popularity.

Tourism is also an important economic sector. The municipality holds various cultural and sports events in the village such as Kabuki show, 'Mishima Yacht Race' and djembe (West African drum) workshops throughout the year to attract tourists.

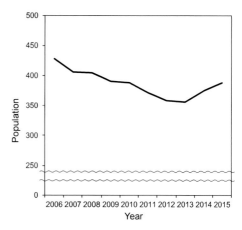

Fig. 3. Population of Mishima-mura (2006-2015). Source: Website of Mishima-mura (in Japanese).

It is notable that the total population in the three villages has increased in the last few years thanks to the collaborative efforts of the villagers and the municipality office as figure 3 shows.

3. Paper in the section: More details of the industry in Amami Islands

The papers in this chapter vary in topics relating to the industrial activities in the islands of Osumi. Regarding agriculture, Masashi Yamamoto explains the fruit trees on Tanega-shima and Yaku-shima, and Sota Yamamoto describes the medicinal plants.

Takashi Torii explores the background and future prospects of the efforts toward the introduction of *Yokowa* (young Bluefin tuna) trolling by the Yaku-shima Fisheries Cooperative Association.

References

Nishiniomote City, Nakatane Town and Minamitane Town 2014. Industrialization Plan in Tanega-shima Region, Kagoshima Prefecture (西之表町，中種子町，南種町 2014．鹿児島県種子島地域産業化計画 2014). (in Japanese)

Yaku Town 2015. Statistics of Yaku-shima (屋久町 2015．平成 27 年度，統計やくしま). (in Japanese)

Websites

Mishima-mura: http://mishimamura.com/ (Accessed on 12 December, 2016, in Japanese).

JAXA: http://global.jaxa.jp/about/jaxa/index.html (Accessed on 12 December, 2016).

Chapter 7
Background and Future Prospects of the Efforts toward the Introduction of *Yokowa* (young bluefin tuna) Trolling by the Yaku-shima Fisheries Cooperative Association

Takashi TORII

1. Abstract

The research project we conducted in 2014 analyzed the outcomes of the efforts made in the Yaku-shima Island to introduce trolling of *yokowa* (young bluefin tuna) and to address future issues.

In 2012, the Yaku-shima Fisheries Cooperative Association received requests from Company A and Company B to harvest *yokowa*. With the knowledge that the Yaku-shima Island had a history of *yokowa* fishing, the Fisheries cooperative association encouraged local fishing operators to obtain the *yokowa* fishing permit; as a result, the operators obtained the permit for 53 fishing vessels. The two companies ordered a total of 5,000 fish, which was expected to bring 17.5 million yen to the island. As the *yokowa* fishing season coincides with the off season of the pole-and-line fishing of shallow water fish, local fishing operators had great expectation for the start of *yokowa* fishing.

However, no *yokowa* was harvested in 2014. As the Western & Central Pacific Fisheries Commission (WCPFC) points out, the bluefin tuna resource in the Pacific Ocean is significantly decreasing. The waters off the coast of Kagoshima Prefecture, where *yokowa* used to be regularly harvested in the past, are no exception. Currently, the possibility of *yokowa* trolling stabilizing the fishery businesses on the Yaku-shima Island is not prospective.

2. Purposes of this study

Recent tightening of regulations related to the use of natural bluefin tuna fries for aquaculture and poor catch of *yokowa* by trolling has worsened the prospect of obtaining bluefin tuna fries used for aquaculture. Under these circumstances, some fish farmers try to secure stable supply of fries by expanding their sources as well as by strengthening business connections1. In contrast, in areas where there is a good chance of *yokowa* harvesting in the surrounding waters, some fishing operators obtained the *yokowa* fishing permit at the time of switchover in April 2014 from the free fishery system to the permit-based system for *yokowa* trolling, aiming to promote the local fishing industry.

In the research project conducted in 2014 using the Yaku-shima Fisheries cooperative association in Kagoshima Prefecture as an example, we analyzed the background, outcomes, and issues surrounding the efforts toward introducing *yokowa* trolling.

3. Outline of the fishing industry in the Yaku-shima Island

The Yaku-shima Fisheries Cooperative Association

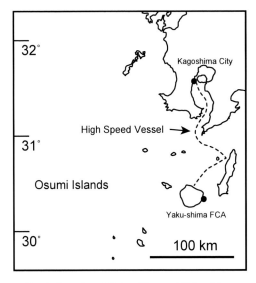

Fig. 1. Location of Yaku-shima and Yaku-shima FCA.

was established in 2004 through the merger of several fisheries cooperative associations on the island. It has 109 regular and 114 associate members (Fig. 1). The main fishing types used by the members are flying fish trolling, pole-and-line fishing of shallow water fish, pole-and-line fishing of mackerels, bottom gill-net fishing, and fishing of *mojako* (young yellowtails). The annual catch in 2013 was approximately 360 million yen (of which 67 million yen were processed through the cooperative system). In concert with the deterioration of their business conditions, the cooperative revised its commissions in 2013. Commissions were calculated for individual business divisions; these calculations were then used to revise the commissions accordingly. The main types of fishing adopted on the island are outlined below:

3.1. Outline of the main fishing types
3.1.1. Pole-and-line fishing of mackerels

Eighteen operators engage in the pole-and-line fishing of mackerels with an annual catch worth approximately 12 million yen. In the past, the mackerels from the Yaku-shima Island, which were shipped mainly to markets in mainland Kagoshima Prefecture, enjoyed some popularity under the name of Yaku-shima Island's kubiore (broken-necked) mackerels. The fishing operators on the island have been adjusting the production of mackerels in order to prevent a significant drop in the prices.

However, mackerel prices are declining after some mainland districts of Kagoshima Prefecture started selling kubiore mackerels. The amount of mackerels shipped from the Yaku-shima Island to mainland Kagoshima Prefecture has significantly declined owing to lowered profits.

Fishing operators engaging in the pole-and-line fishing of mackerels have had little choice but to send the fish to markets on the island; however, owing to the small market size of the island, production adjustments have been introduced, e.g., 20 fish per vessel for one-person vessels and 30 fish per vessel for two-person vessels. As a result of the adjustments, the per-kilo price has been maintained between 800 yen and 1,000 yen.

The demand for mackerels tends to increase in summer (June to August) when the number of tourists increases. However, temporal farming of mackerels is not possible at this time of the year owing to higher water temperature, thus preventing steady supply of the fish during the season. In contrast, in winter, mackerels can be farmed for 3 to 4 days, providing a stable supply of fish, but the lower number of tourists decreases the demand for the fish in this season. For these reasons, the Fisheries cooperative association has been repeatedly conducting quick-freezing tests jointly with local fishery product processors. With the high prospect of completing this technology, near-fresh mackerels are expected to be supplied to the island market in summers in the near future.

3.1.2. Pole-and-line fishing of shallow water fish

Catches are not stable between April and June of every year. After early May, whereas mackerel catches stabilize, catches of other shallow water fish are generally poor.

The main target fish include sea breams and mackerels in shallow waters and Japanese butterfish and rosy snappers in deep waters. Shibi2 and skipjack tuna are also harvested, but they are intended mainly for self-consumption owing to low prices.

The fishing grounds for Japanese butterfish and rosy snappers are far from the island – near the Tokara Islands – and fishing operators operate for two to four nights by either staying on the sea or at accommodations on the Nakanoshima Island or the Kuchinoshima Island to save time and fuel. Despite being combined, the *hatanagashi* (long free-floating dropline) fishing of swordfish, trolling of skipjack tuna, pufferfish fishing, and bait fishing of red sea breams and yellow jacks, the overall catch has been on the decline in the past few years.

The catches from day operations are sold mainly on the Yaku-shima Island, and the catches from overnight operations are mainly sent to the markets in mainland Kagoshima Prefecture. Vessels return to their ports on a pre-arranged day and the catches are jointly shipped to mainland Kagoshima Prefecture in a container.

3.1.3. Fishing of *mojako*

Since around 1985, fishing operators with a special fishing permit have engaged in *mojako* fishing3 on the island. Four operators joined in 2004 raising the total number of *mojako* fishing operators to 23.

Normally, *mojako* fishing starts around April 10 and ends at the end of the month. In the past, mainly the operators from the Isso District practiced *mojako* fishing. In the Anbo District, however, operators did not engage in *mojako* fishing because flying fish trolling was thriving in the district. However, as the business conditions of the flying fish trolling deteriorated, six local vessels in the Anbo District commenced *mojako* fishing.

In recent years, it has been observed that the size of caught *mojako* fish has increased. Additionally, the *mojako* harvest season is arriving earlier than before. The Cooperative believes that these changes are partly due to the rise in sea water temperature. In 2014, seaweeds started drifting in early March bringing together *mojako*. Drifting seaweeds were still seen in April but did not contain as many *mojako* as they used to in March. The Cooperative insisted to move the fishing season to an earlier date, but the decision was not made until recently owing to reasons such as lack of fish preservation capacity on the reception side. In 2014, the fishing season was expected to start on April 5.

The per kilo price of *mojako* used to be approximately 30,000 yen, but currently, it ranges between 8,000 yen and 10,000 yen. The current annual catch of *mojako* is worth approximately 6 million yen, which is 60% of its value in the past.

Furthermore, in 2012 the *Beko* disease[4] appeared. In 2013, the fish were farmed unless they got infected with *Microsporidium seriolae*, but the disease did not occur. In 2014, the disease was not present during farming but appeared after transportation to farming places. Morbidity rate varies depending on where *mojako* are temporarily farmed on the island and how to address this warrants further consideration.

3.1.4. Trolling of flying fish

In districts under the control of the Yaku-shima Fisheries cooperative association, flying fish were harvested in the past by combining several fishing methods such as drift net fishing in winter and offshore set-net fishing in spring. However, after the war, fishing operators who left the Yoronjima Island looking for flying fish fishing grounds and settled in the Anbo District via Itoman in Okinawa Prefecture devised a trolling method by improving the drive fishing method. The trolling method became locally widespread due to its efficiency. Thus, the flying fish trolling in the Yaku-shima Island was developed by migrants. This is a type of surrounding gill net fishing carried out by two vessels (the main and the second vessel) as a team, and it is characterized by the use of ropes to drive fish instead of large meshed nets and wing nets.

There are cases where one owner or one family owns both the main and second vessels, but in many cases, two owners jointly operate. The owner of the main vessel owns the necessary equipment including machinery and fish boxes, whereas the owner of the second vessel simply assists the main vessel during the operations. As the chief fisherman, the owner of the main vessel assumes command of choosing fishing grounds, navigating the vessels, etc. All but one mariner (the owner of the second vessel) board the main vessel and engage in net casting, hauling, and fish sorting. The waters surrounding the Taneyaku Straight are good fishing grounds for flying fish, with a branch current of the Kuroshio Current flowing in all year round, which creates upwelling and thereby stabilizing the water temperature and creating a plankton-friendly environment. These waters enjoy steady visits of diverse flying fish resources all year round, and flying fish species harvested in these waters vary depending on the season. While it is common to repeat a one-hour haul five or six times per day, in times of bumper catches, the number of hauls may be reduced by all operating vessels to prevent price collapsing; overall, the work intensity is not too high. Vessels can set their own departure time, but since there is a rule that all vessels must complete catch landing return by 3 PM, most vessels leave their ports at dawn and end the operation between noon and 3

PM. To adjust the production, the number of days vessels operate in a year (120–150 days) is not high.

Flying fish trolling used to be conducted by a fleet of two vessels with four or five mariners. Currently, it is still conducted by a fleet of two vessels but typically with three mariners. Since the owners struggle to pay their mariners sufficiently, the number of mariners participating in this type of fishing is decreasing. Furthermore, operators are leaving the industry one after another; in the Anbo District, where flying fish trolling is active, a total of 14 fleets were operating in 2004, whereas only eight fleets were active in 2014.

Some of the operators engaging in flying fish trolling started providing tourist services. Such operators have registered their vessels as recreational fishing vessels; they purchased the required equipment with subsidies from Kagoshima Prefecture and are expected to provide tourists staying in the Anbo District with marine leisure activities.

3.2. Current status of fishery management where multiple fishing types are combined

Fishery operators run their businesses by combining multiple aforementioned fishing methods. Of the 53 *yokowa* fishing operators, who will be addressed later in this paper, 23 also engage in *mojako* fishing. Furthermore, it is a common practice for operators to combine their usual fishing methods with the pole-and-line fishing of the seasonal fish.

How operators combine fishing types varies depending on the area of the island. Operators in the Isso District engage mainly in day operations, targeting mackerels and shallow water fish. Operators in the Kurio District also engage mainly in day operations, but target deep water fish. Many operators in the Anbo District catch deep water fish such as Japanese butterfish and rosy snappers, and flying fish.

One of the challenges associated with running a fishery business in the Yaku-shima Island is distribution. In the past, Iwasaki Ferry operated ferries that would leave the island at 4:30 AM for mainland Kagoshima Prefecture. Using these services, it was possible to send fish to Tokyo on the day of catch. Thus, the Yaku-shima Fisheries cooperative association would send fish to the Tokyo Central Wholesale Market, where higher prices were expected compared to prices offered at markets in mainland Kagoshima Prefecture.

However, the ferry route was abolished in 2011 and the ferries, currently operated by Orita Kisen, leave the island at 1:30 PM and arrive at mainland Kagoshima Prefecture at 5:40 PM. If these services are used, fish will arrive in Tokyo on the next day of catch, creating a significant disadvantage for the Cooperative in terms of fish freshness.

If airmail is used, the shipping from the Yaku-shima Island to mainland Kagoshima Prefecture costs between 350 yen/kg and 380 yen/kg (Japan Air Commuter) and the shipping from mainland Kagoshima Prefecture to Tokyo costs 110 yen/kg (Nippon Express's airmail service), incurring the total cost of approximately 500 yen/kg, thereby limiting the shipping of profitable fish species.

4. Challenges of the *yokowa* trolling introduction

4.1. Background

While the business conditions remained largely weak, in 2012 the Cooperative was contacted by Company A and Company B who wanted to secure fishing of *yokowa*[5].

Yokowa weighing approximately 1 kg had been caught in the waters surrounding the Yaku-shima Island, whereas in the Isso District, *yokowa* were caught as bycatch of bullet tuna fisheries between January and March. Therefore, the Cooperative determined that it would be possible to catch *yokowa* in the waters near the island and encouraged local operators to obtain the permit for *yokowa* trolling. Subsequently, 53 vessels obtained the required permit, which became mandatory in April 2014.

4.2. Plan

According to the plan, after the completion of *mojako* fishing, *yokowa* would be caught between June and July, temporarily farmed in an acclimation reservoir installed near the entrance to the Isso Port (5 m deep) for 5 to 7 days, and transported using a live fish vessel. Because the migration routes of *yokowa* are not clearly known, 1.5 million yen from the Remote Island Fisheries Revitalization Subsidy Program would be used to search the fishing grounds. It was agreed that Company A and Company B would purchase *yokowa* at 3,500 yen per fish.

4.3. Outcomes and issues

In early May 2014, approximately 10 fishing operators hosted a technical training course at Company A. Installation of the fish reservoir and preparation of fishing gear such as depressors, among others, were accelerated with anticipation of great *yokowa* catch, since the technique used was similar to that used for bullet tuna fishing.

Four or five fishing vessels searched *yokowa* resources. Although fishing operators in the Yakushima Island had not conducted *yokowa* fishing between late June and late July, they knew from experience that *yokowa* visit the northern limit of the Kuroshio Current. The operators from the Isso District searched the northern end of the Kuroshio Current and the operators from the Anbo District searched on the hither side of the Kuroshio Current. However, *yokowa* was not caught in 2014 and much of the 1.5 million yen secured for this project remained unused. From the long-term perspective, the Cooperative, fishing operators, Company A, and Company B intend to continue with this project. In 2015, search for *yokowa* resources started in May after the completion of *mojako* fishing.

Additionally, the Cooperative has made a request to the Kagoshima Prefectural Government to create a breakwater off the Isso Port (water depth 27 m). Currently, domestic wastewater and rainwater flow into the acclimation reservoir as it is located inside the bay. To create the reservoir in a sea area that is not affected by these waters, a breakwater needs to be built to protect the reservoir from the waves. Considering the cost of the construction and the fact that coral reef is widely distributed in these waters, the prospect of breakwater construction is currently not clear.

4.4. Future prospects

Company A and Company B ordered a total of 5,000 fish. If the number is successfully sold, 17.5 million yen will be shared by 53 fishing operators, which corresponds to about 330,000 yen per operator. The fishing operators do not have to pay for fuel as it is covered by the Remote Island Fisheries Revitalization Subsidy Program.

Additionally, the local fishing operators have great expectation for *yokowa* trolling as the *yokowa* harvest season coincides with the off season of pole-and-line fishing for shallow water fish.

Acknowledgment

Part of this work was supported by JSPS KAKENHI Grant Number 15K07614.

Chapter 8
Fruit Trees on Tanega-shima and Yaku-shima

Masashi YAMAMOTO

1. Introduction

Tanega-shima and Yaku-shima are located at a latitude of approximately 30 degrees north (Fig. 1). Areas of Tanega-shima and Yaku-shima are 444.5 and 504.3 km^2, being the second and third largest islands in Kagoshima Prefecture, respectively. Although the regions and areas of the islands are similar, their geographic features are quite different. Tanega-shima is very flat and the highest point above sea level is only 282 m, whereas the highest peak of Yaku-shima, Miyanouradake, reaches an altitude of 1,936 m. Winter on both islands is mild (Fig. 2) since they are located south of Kyushu. Yaku-shima has an annual rainfall of about 4,500 millimeters, the highest amount in Japan (Fig. 3).

2. Fruits production on Tanega-shima and Yaku-shima

Various agricultural crops adapted to a warm climate have been cultivated on both islands. On Tanega-shima, sugarcane, sweet potato, and rice, cultivated in flatlands, are major crops. In comparison with these major crops, fruit production on the island is not so active. On the other hand, the main agricultural crop on Yaku-shima is fruit, especially citrus. It is mainly cultivated along the shoreline since high mountains are located at the center of the island.

Table 1 shows fruit production on Tanega-

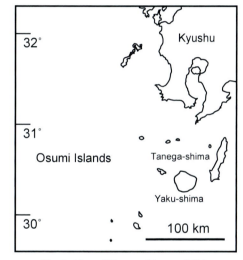

Fig. 1. Map of Tanega-shima and Yaku-shima.

Table 1. Production area (ha) of fruit trees on Tanega-shima and Yaku-shima (2013).

Island	Citrus				Loquat	Mango	Passion fruit
	Satsuma mandarin	Ponkan	Tankan	Shiranui			
Tanega-shima	0.2	27.0	26.3	0.0	0.3	2.1	1.3
Yaku-shima	0.5	115.0	232.0	0.2	4.0	1.5	7.9
Total	0.7	142.0	258.3	0.2	4.3	3.6	9.2
Kagoshima Pref.	959.7	504.5	662.6	181.0	151.5	65.3	38.2

Modified from Kagoshima Prefecture (2015).

shima and Yaku-shima. In citrus, Ponkan (*Citrus reticulata* BLANCO) and Tankan (*Citrus tankan* HAYATA) are the most important (Fig. 4). Since both species are adapted to a warm climate, fruit of a good quality can be produced on both islands. Yaku-shima is very famous for these citrus, and they are specialty products on both islands. However, the production of Satsuma mandarin (*Citrus unshiu* MARC.), a leading citrus cultivar in Japan, is very limited on both islands since a cool

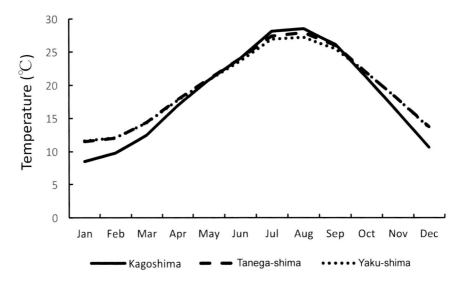

Fig. 2. Monthly average temperature of Kagoshima, Tanega-shima, and Yaku-shima.

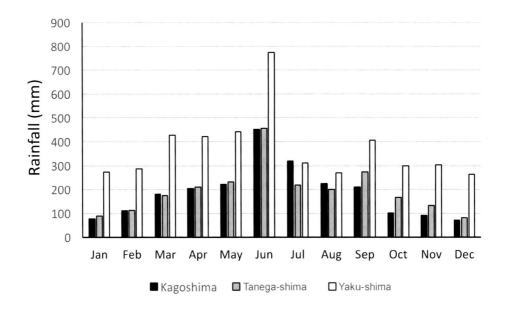

Fig. 3. Monthly rainfall for Kagoshima, Tanega-shima, and Yaku-shima.

Fig. 4. Major citrus on Tanega-shima and Yaku-shima. Left: Tankan (*Citrus tankan*) of Yaku-shima, right: Ponkan (*C. reticulata*) of Tanega-shima.

Fig. 5. Mango (*Mangifera indica*) cultivation under greenhouse conditions (Tanega-shima).

autumn season is essential for its high-quality production. Besides citrus, the evergreen fruit loquat (*Eriobotrya japonica* (THUMB.) LINDTL.), tropical fruit mango (*Mangifera indica* L.), and passion fruit (*Passiflora edulis* SIMS) are cultivated on a small scale (Table 1). Mango and passion fruit are cultivated under greenhouse conditions (Fig. 5).

3. Local citrus grown on Tanega-shima and Yaku-shima

Although the above-mentioned fruit crops cultivated commercially are introduced ones, there are indigenous citrus accessions on Tanega-shima and Yaku-shima. Local citrus, Kuro-shima Mikan (*Citrus* sp.) and Kozu (*Citrus* sp.) (Fig. 6), can be found in backyards or very small scale orchards.

Kuro-shima Mikan is a small fruit mandarin. The characteristics of Kuro-shima Mikan (Table 2) are similar to those of Sakurajima Komikan (*Citrus kinokuni* hort. ex TANAKA). However, its flavor and seed morphology are completely different from Sakurajima Komikan. Moreover, Kuro-shima Mikan could be distinguished from Sakurajima Komikan by DNA analysis. DNA analysis also revealed genetic similarity between Kuro-shima Mikan and Shimamikan (*Citrus* sp.) on Amami Oshima (Yamamoto unpublished). The peel of immature fruit of Kuro-shima Mikan is a popular seasoning on these islands.

Kozu is also a small fruit mandarin. Some types of Kozu are grown on Tanega-shima and Yaku-shima. In this review, two types are described (Fig. 6, Table 2). The taste of all Kozu is not favored since the fruit contains abundant acid. In limited orchards of Tanega-shima, Kozu is used as a rootstock for Tankan to improve tree vigor (Fig. 7).

References

Kagoshima Prefecture 2015. Statistics of Fruit Production (2013). pp. 69, Kagoshima Prefecture, Kagoshima.

Fig. 6. Pictures of local citrus grown on Tanega-shima and Yaku-shima. A, Kuro-shima Mikan (*Citrus* sp.); B, Kozu (*Citrus* sp.) type A; and C, Kozu type B.

Table 2. Leaf and fruit characteristics of Kuroshima Mikan and Kozu (*Citrus* spp.)

Common name	Leaf					Fruit										Seed		
	Leaf blade		Wing		Skin color	Fruit surface	Flavor	Flesh color	Puffing	Granu-lation	Peeling	Diameter (mm)	Height (mm)	D/H index	Brix	Titratable acid (%)	Embryo color	Poly/mono-embryony	Number
	Length (mm)	Width (mm)	Length (mm)	Width (mm)															
Kuroshima Mikan	92.3	38.3	6.0	2.2	Orange	Slightly smooth	Shima Mikan	Orange	None	None	Easy	52.1	35.6	146.3	8.5	1.4	Pale green, Green	Poly	14.3
Kozu type A	105.4	44.4	5.9	2.4	Deep orange	Slightly smooth	-	Orange	None	None	Easy	45.0	30.8	146.1	11.2	4.3	Pale green, Green	Poly	9.0
Kozu type B	83.1	30.6	5.1	2.0	Yellowish orange	Smooth	-	Orange	None	None	Easy	35.2	24.6	143.1	10.5	3.6	Pale green, Green	Poly	9.2

Fig. 7. Kozu (*Citrus* sp.) used as a rootstock for Tankan.

Chapter 9
Medicinal Plants of Tanega-shima and Yaku-shima Islands

Sota YAMAMOTO

1. Introduction

Traditional medicines or remedies, which are based on traditional knowledge transmitted from generation to generation, are very important for local people living on small and especially remote islands in the Asia-Pacific region. They are essential for these populations as they enable them to live healthy and happily because of limited transportation and a poor environment for modern medical practices. Moreover, plants used for traditional medicines have great potential for modern medication as useful compounds, which are often identified to treat specific diseases.

In the Nansei Islands of Japan, there are many islands arranged in a "stepping-stones" pattern from north to south. These islands include many different types of habitats, climates, languages, cultures, etc. In such a region, we can explore the similarity and dissimilarity of plant usage to understand the historical movement of local peoples, the transmission of traditional knowledge, and the introduction of new plants. YAMAMOTO (2016) studied the medicinal plants of Tokuno-shima Island in the Amami Islands, but there are very few English articles on the traditional medicines or remedies of the Osumi Islands. This chapter focuses on medicinal plants and traditional remedies drawn from plants found on both Tanega-shima and Yaku-shima islands.

2. Tanega-shima Island

2.1. Nishinoomote City (referred from Nishinoomote Hensan Iinkai [1971])

Common cold: A decoction of the dried leaves of *Artemisia* spp. and *Plantago asiatica* is taken; the juice of the peel of *Citrus unshiu* is taken; a decoction of the roots of *Zingiber officinale* is taken.

Diarrhea: A decoction of the bark of *Elaeagnus* spp. is taken.

Hemostasis: The leaves of *Artemisia* spp. are applied.

Ichthyism: Liquid squeezed from the leaves and stems of *Farfugium japonicum* is taken.

Myositis: The bulb of *Narcissus* spp. is helpful in the treatment of myositis (no detailed method of use is provided).

Neuralgia: A decoction of the wood of *Morus* spp. is taken with some iron.

Stomachaches/gastrointestinal disorders: Liquid from the leaves of *Artemisia* spp. is taken; a decoction of the roots of *Curcuma zedoaria* is taken; a decoction of the bark of *Elaeagnus* spp. is taken; a decoction of *Geranium thunbergii* is taken; liquid from the squeezed leaves of *Rubus sieboldii* is taken.

Swollen parts and boils: Liquid from the leaves of *Crinum asiaticum* is applied; the toasted leaves of *F. japonicum* are applied.

Tetanus: A decoction of the wood of *Diospyros kaki* is taken with sticky rice, the roasted shells of shrimp, and other additives.

Urticarial: The fruits of *Canarium album* are eaten.

Wounds: The oil of *Acorus calamus* is applied; the fruits of *Cycas revoluta* are applied; the resin of *Pinus* spp. is applied.

2.2. Nakatane Town (referred from Nakatanechou Kyoudo Henshuu Iinkai [1971] and Department of Anthropology, Faculty of Law, Economics and Humanities, Kagoshima University [1984])

Burns: The bark of *Prunus* subg. *Cerasus* spp. (no detailed method of use is provided).

Cough medicine and medicine that promotes expectoration: *Fortunella* spp. (no detailed method of use is provided).

Diarrhea: A decoction of *G. thunbergii* is taken for diarrhea or dysentery.

Eye injury/disease: Sap from the stems of *Vitis* spp. is used as eye drops.

Filariasis: A mixture of the wood of *Buxus microphylla*, the roots of *H. cordata*, the roots of *Smilax* spp., etc. (no detailed method of use is provided).

Kidney disease: *Cirsium* spp. (no detailed method of use is provided); the male inflorescence of *Zea mays* (no detailed method of use is provided).

Otorrhea: Liquid from the squeezed leaves of *Houttuynia cordata* is applied.

Poor blood circulation: *Oenanthe javanica* (no detailed method of use is provided).

Skin diseases, ringworm, scabies, etc.: *Agave* spp. is effective at treating rashes caused by fertilizer (no detailed method of use is provided); the fruits of *Gardenia jasminoides* are used for chapped hands; the resin of *Pinus* spp. is applied.

Stomachaches/gastrointestinal disorders: *Aloe arborescens* (no detailed method of use is provided); liquid from the squeezed leaves of *Artemisia* spp. is taken; the leaf buds of *Clerodendrum trichotomum* (no detailed method of use is provided); *C. zedoaria* (no detailed method of use is provided); *Swertia japonica* (no detailed method of use is provided).

Swollen parts and boils: *Allium tuberosum* (no detailed method of use is provided); the leaves of *F. japonicum* are applied with roasted shrimp shells; the toasted leaves of *F. japonicum* are applied; the leaves of *H. cordata* are applied; the bulbs of *Narcissus* spp. are applied; the leaves of *P. asiatica* are applied; the squeezed leaves of *S. japonica* are applied.

Tetanus: *F. japonicum* leaves (no detailed method of use is provided).

Toxicosis: The leaves, stems, and fruits of *C. album* (no detailed method of use is provided); *H. cordata* (no detailed method of use is provided).

Vermifuge: *Digenea simplex* (no detailed method of use is provided); a decoction of the bark of *Melia azedarach* is taken; *Punica granatum* (no detailed method of use is provided).

Warts: A decoction of the fruits of *Coix lacryma-jobi* is taken; a decoction of *H. cordata* is taken; slices of the fruit of *Solanum melongena* are rubbed on the afflicted area.

Wounds: *Artemisia* spp. (no detailed method of use is provided); the ground stems of *C. revoluta* are placed on the injured area (when you step on a nail).

2.3. Minamitane Town (referred from Minamitanechou Kyoudoshi Hensan Iinkai [1987])

Bites by poisonous snakes (*mamushi*), bees, centipedes, etc.: Steam from the leaves of *Cryptomeria japonica* are applied to the injured area (notably snake bites); the fruits of *Cucurbita* spp. are eaten after a poisonous snake bite; liquid from the fruits of *Luffa cylindrica* is applied to the injury (notably bee and centipede stings).

Burns: The charred bark of *Prunus* subg. *Cerasus* spp. is mixed with seed oil and applied.

Common cold: A decoction of the leaves of *Cinnamomum camphora* is taken; a decoction of the fruit peel of *Citrus natsudaidai* is taken; liquid from the squeezed fresh leaves (or from the whole plant) of *Saxifraga stolonifera* is taken.

Cough medicine and medicine that promotes expectoration: A decoction of the fruit peel of *C. natsudaidai* is taken for hoarseness.

Diarrhea: Liquid of the squeezed leaves of *C. trichotomum* is taken for dysentery; a decoction of *G. thunbergii* is taken for diarrhea or dysentery; liquid from the fruits of *Prunus mume* that have been soaked in sea water is taken for diarrhea.

Eye injury/disease: Steam from green tea (*Camellia sinensis*) are placed over the eyes; sap from the stems of *Vitis* spp. is used as eye drops.

Hemostasis: The squeezed leaves of *Hydrocotyle sibthorpioides* are applied.

Skin diseases, ringworm, scabies, etc.: The toasted shoots of *Arundo donax* are rubbed on rashes caused by fertilizer; the dried and pounded leaves of *C. sinensis* are applied to area infected with ringworm; the dried beans of *Glycine max* are applied to the fingers infected with ringworm; liquid containing *Ipomoea batatas* broth is applied to rashes caused by fertilizer; the squeezed fresh flowers of *Lonicera japonica* are applied to heat rashes; liquid from the fruits of *L. cylindrica* is applied to heat rashes.

Stomachaches/gastrointestinal disorders: The squeezed leaves of *Artemisia* spp. dissolved in hot water are taken; a decoction of the dried roots and stems of *Cirsium* spp. is taken; a decoction of the dried slices the roots of *C. zedoaria* is taken; a powder made from the dried roots of *C. zedoaria* is taken with water; the fresh leaves of *F. japonicum* are eaten; a decoction of *G. thunbergii* is taken; the salted fruits of *P. mume* are eaten.

Swollen parts and boils: The toasted leaves of *F. japonicum* are applied; the squeezed leaves of *H. cordata* are applied; a decoction of the roots of *P. asiatica* is taken; the squeezed fresh leaves of *P. asiatica* are applied.

Tooth disease: The squeezed leaves of *Artemisia* spp. are applied to the decayed tooth; the tar in the smoke of tobacco (*Nicotiana* spp.) that accumulates in a pipe is applied to the decayed tooth.

Toxicosis: A decoction of the leaves and branches of *C. album* is taken to remedy food poisoning; a decoction of the leaves of *D. kaki* is taken to remedy food poisoning; the salted fruits of *P. mume* are eaten to remedy food poisoning.

Vermifuge: Liquid from the squeezed leaves of *Artemisia* spp. with salt is taken; a decoction of the dried plant portion of *D. simplex* is taken.

Wounds: The squeezed leaves of *A. tuberosum* are applied; the dried leaves of *Artemisia* spp. are burnt on the injured area (moxibustion); steam from the leaves of *Cryptomeria japonica* is applied; the squeezed leaves of *Cryptomeria japonica* are applied; flour made from *Fagopyrum esculentum* are applied to the injured area (when you step on bamboo); the squeezed leaves of *F. japonicum* are applied; the toasted leaves of *H. cordata* are applied; the squeezed leaves of *Impatiens balsamina* are applied.

3. Yaku-shima Island (referred from HIROSE [1987], Department of Anthropology, Faculty of Law, Economics and Humanities, Kagoshima University [1989], and Yakuchou Kyoudoshi Hensan Iinkai [1993, 1995, 2003])

3.1. Nagakubo

Bites by poisonous snakes (*mamushi*), bees, centipedes, etc.: Liquid from *A. arborescens* is applied to the injured area after an insect or snake bite.

Constipation: *H. cordata* (no detailed method of use is provided).

Cough medicine and medicine promoting expectoration: *Lilium lancifolium* for cough medicine (no detailed method of use is provided); *P. asiatica* for cough medicine (no detailed method of use is provided).

Cystitis: *P. asiatica* (no detailed method of use is provided).

Diarrhea: *G. thunbergii* (no detailed method of use is provided).

Empyema: *H. cordata* (no detailed method of use is provided).

Eye injury/disease: *P. asiatica* for bloodshot eyes (no detailed method of use is provided); sap from the stems of *Vitis* spp. is used as eye drops.

Neuralgia: Liquid from *Cirsium* spp. roots soaked in liquor (*shouchuu*) is taken.

Stomachaches/gastrointestinal disorders: A decoction of *G. thunbergii* is taken; liquid from the salted fruits of *P. mume* is taken.

Swollen parts and boils: The steamed fresh leaves of *H. cordata* are applied.

Vermifuge: A decoction of the root bark from of *M. azedarach* is taken.

Wounds: The squeezed leaves of *Artemisia* spp. are applied.

3.2. Funayuki

Antipyretic: The grated bulbs of *Lycoris radiata* are applied to the soles of the feet.

Diarrhea: A decoction of dried *G. thunbergii* is taken.

Eye injury/disease: Sap from the stems of *Vitis* spp. is used as eye drops; liquid from the roots of *Zingiber mioga* is applied to the injured area.

Heartburn: Fresh *F. japonicum* leaves are chewed.

Hemostasis: The squeezed leaves of *Artemisia* spp. are applied; the squeezed leaves of *H. sibthorpioides* are applied.

Hypertension: A cup of the squeezed leaves of *Artemisia* spp. is taken before breakfast.

Kidney disease: A decoction of the dried male inflorescence of *Z. mays* is taken.

Otorrhea: Liquid from the squeezed leaves of *S. stolonifera* is poured into the ear.

Stomachaches/gastrointestinal disorders: A decoction of dried slices (fresh slices for emergencies) of the roots of *C. zedoaria* is taken; a decoction of the dried plant portion of *G. thunbergii* is taken.

Swollen parts and boils: A mixture of the charred leaves of *F. japonicum*, charred shrimp shells, and cooked rice are applied; the toasted leaves of *H. cordata* are applied.

Toxicosis: A decoction of the dried plant portion of *H. cordata* is taken.

3.3. Matsumine

Accidental ingestion: When you swallow a nail accidentally, you should eat the fried leaves (cut into long sections) of *A. tuberosum*, which will entwine the nail in the stomach and both the leaves and the nail will come out together.

Antipyretic: A decoction of the dried branches of *Elaeagnus* spp. is taken.

Bites by poisonous snakes (*mamushi*), bees, centipedes, etc.: Liquid from *A. arborescens* is applied to an injury caused by a centipede or bee sting; liquid from the stems of *Colocasia esculenta* is applied to an injury caused by a bee sting.

Burns: A decoction of the bark of *Prunus* subg. *Cerasus* spp. is applied.

Common cold: A decoction of the dried plant portion of *P. asiatica* is taken.

Diarrhea: *G. thunbergii* (no detailed method of use is provided).

Eye injury/disease: Sap from the stems of *Vitis* spp. is used as eye drops.

Hemostasis: Liquid from *A. arborescens* is applied; the squeezed leaves of *Artemisia* spp. are applied; the squeezed leaves of *H. sibthorpioides* are applied; the dried leaves of *Nicotiana* spp. are applied.

Hypertension: A decoction of the dried plant portion of *P. asiatica* is taken.

Neuralgia: A person soaks in bathwater with *Artemisia* spp. leaves; a decoction of the dried leaves of *D. kaki*, the dried stems and leaves of *Gynostemma pentaphyllum*, and the leaves of *Limonium* spp. is taken.

Skin diseases, ringworm, scabies, etc.: The dried leaves of *C. sinensis* are applied to the fingers infected with ringworm.

Stomachaches/gastrointestinal disorders: *Allium sativum* (no detailed method of use is provided); *A. arborescens* (no detailed method of use is provided); *Artemisia* spp. (no detailed method of use is provided); a decoction of the dried plant portion of *G. thunbergii* is taken; *H. cordata* (no detailed method of use is provided); *Lycium chinense* (no detailed method of use is provided); *P. asiatica* (no detailed method of use is provided).

Wounds: A mixture of the charred leaves of *F. japonicum*, charred shrimp shells, and cooked rice is applied.

3.4. Anbou

Accidental ingestion: When you swallow a nail or needle accidentally, you should eat the fried leaves (cut into long sections) of *A. tuberosum*, which will entwine the nail or needle in the stomach and both the leaves and the nail will come out together.

Asthma: Liquid from the plant portion of *A. arborescens* soaked in liquor (*shouchuu*) is taken; *P. asiatica* (no detailed method of use is provided).

Bites by poisonous snakes (*mamushi*), bees, centipedes, etc.: Liquid from the plant portion of *A. arborescens* is applied to the insect bite; liquid from the stems of *C. esculenta* is applied to the injury/insect bite.

Burns: Liquid from the plant portion of *A. arborescens* is applied.

Cancer: A decoction of *Pseudosasa owatarii* is taken.

Constipation: The cooked roots of *I. batatas* are eaten.

Diabetes: Roasted or deep fried shoots of *Aralia elata* are eaten; a decoction of the stems and roots of *A. elata* is taken; a decoction of the dried leaves of *D. kaki* is taken; a decoction of the dried leaves of *Eriobotrya japonica* is taken; a decoction of *P. owatarii* is taken; a decoction of the dried leaves of *Psidium* spp. is taken.

Diarrhea: A decoction of the dried plant portion of *G. thunbergii* is taken.

Diuretic: The fruits of *Citrullus lanatus* are eaten; a decoction of the dried male inflorescence of *Z. mays* is taken.

Eye injury/disease: Sap from the stems of *Vitis* spp. is used as eye drops.

Fatigue recovery: Grated or toasted bulbs of *A. sativum* are eaten.

Gynecopathy: A decoction of the dried leaves of *D. kaki* is taken; a decoction of the dried plant portion of *G. thunbergii* is taken; a decoction of the dried leaves and stems of *H. cordata* is taken; a decoction of the dried leaves and stems of *P. asiatica* is taken.

Heartburn: A decoction of the roots of *C. zedoaria* is taken; the boiled stems of *F. japonicum* are eaten; a powder made from the dried stems of *F. japonicum* is taken with water; the fresh leaves of *Pinus* spp. are chewed.

Hemostasis: The squeezed leaves of *Artemisia* spp. are applied; the squeezed leaves of *H. sibthorpioides* are applied.

Hypertension: A decoction of the dried leaves of *D. kaki* is taken; a decoction of the dried leaves of *E. japonica* is taken; liquid from *E. japonica* leaves soaked in liquor (*shouchuu*) is taken; a decoction of *G. pentaphyllum* is taken; the fresh leaves of *Perilla frutescens* are cut into small pieces and eaten; a decoction of the dried plant portion of *P. asiatica* is taken; a decoction of the dried leaves of *Psidium* spp. is taken.

Kidney disease: The pickled rind of *C. lanatus* is eaten.

Neuralgia: Liquid squeezed from *Artemisia* spp. leaves is taken; liquid from the dried leaves of *Limonium* spp. soaked in liquor (*shouchuu*) is taken.

Otorrhea: Liquid from the squeezed leaves of *Artemisia* spp. is poured into the ear; liquid from the squeezed leaves of *S. stolonifera* is poured into the ear.

Skin diseases, ringworm, scabies, etc.: The grated roots of *Phytolacca* spp. are mixed with vinegar and then applied.

Sprains/fractures/bruises: The grated tubers of *C. esculenta* are applied to the sprain and bandaged; the grated roots of *Raphanus sativus* are applied to the fracture to relieve pain.

Stomachaches/gastrointestinal disorders: Liquid from the plant portion of *A. arborescens* is taken; roasted or deep fried shoots of *A. elata* are eaten; a decoction of the stems and roots of *A. elata* is taken; liquid squeezed from the leaves of *Artemisia* spp. is taken; a decoction of the roots of *C. zedoaria* is taken; a powder made from dried roots of *C. zedoaria* is taken with water; a decoction of the dried plant portion of *G. thunbergii* is taken; the fresh leaves of *P. frutescens* are cut into small pieces and eaten; the fresh leaves of *Pinus* spp. are chewed; a decoction of *P. owatarii* is taken.

Swollen parts and boils: The toasted leaves of *Alocasia odora* are applied; the toasted leaves of *C. asiaticum* are applied; the toasted leaves of *F. japonicum* are applied; the squeezed leaves of *H. cordata* are applied; the toasted leaves of *Lilium maculatum* are applied.

Toxicosis: The boiled stems of *F. japonicum* are eaten; a powder made from the dried stems of *F. japonicum* is taken with water; a decoction of the dried leaves of *H. cordata* is taken;

liquid from the squeezed fresh leaves of *H. cordata* are mixed with honey and taken; a decoction of the dried plant portion of *P. asiatica* is taken.

Vermifuge: A decoction of the dried plant portion of *D. simplex* is taken.

Wounds: Liquid of the squeezed leaves of *Artemisia* spp. is applied; the charred stems of *C. revoluta* are kneaded with cooked rice and applied to the injured area (when you step on a nail); the squeezed leaves and flowers of *I. balsamina* are applied.

3.5. Harumaki

Accidental ingestion: When a fish bone is stuck in your throat, you should drink grated bulbs of *Allium chinense* dissolved in hot water and proceed by vomiting up the solution.

Antipyretic: Liquid from the squeezed fresh leaves of *Artemisia* spp. (sometimes mixed with sap from the stems of *Musa* spp. and brown sugar) is taken.

Asthma: A decoction of the dried fruits of *Trichosanthes* spp. is taken.

Bites by poisonous snakes (*mamushi*), bees, centipedes, etc.: Liquid from the plant portion of *A. arborescens* is applied to the insect bite; liquid from the stems of *C. esculenta* is applied to the insect bite.

Burns: Liquid from the plant portion of *A. arborescens* is applied; the grated tubers of *Solanum tuberosum* are applied.

Cancer: The grated bulbs of *Crocosmia* x *crocosmiiflora* are dissolved in hot water and taken; a decoction of the dried plant portion of *P. owatarii* is taken.

Common cold: A decoction of the dried peel of *C. unshiu* is taken; liquid from the charred salted fruits of *P. mume* are dissolved in hot water and taken.

Cough medicine and medicine promoting expectoration: A decoction of the dried fruits of *Elaeagnus* spp. is taken.

Diarrhea: Liquid from the squeezed plant portion of *A. arborescens* is taken; a decoction of the dried fruits of *Elaeagnus* spp. is taken; a decoction of the dried plant portion of *G. thunbergii* is taken.

Diuretic: The fruits of *C. lanatus* are eaten; a decoction of the dried plant portion of *P. asiatica* is taken.

Eye injury/disease: A bulb of *A. tuberosum* is wiped around the eyes to relieve eyestrain; sap from the stems of *Vitis* spp. is used as eye drops.

Gynecopathy: A decoction of fresh *E. japonica* leaves is taken.

Heartburn: The fresh plant portion of *F. japonicum* is chewed.

Heart disease: The leaves of *Gynura bicolor* are eaten every day.

Hemostasis: The squeezed leaves of *Artemisia* spp. are applied; the squeezed leaves of *H. sibthorpioides* are applied.

Hypertension: A decoction of fresh *D. kaki* leaves is taken.

Kidney disease: A decoction of the dried male inflorescence of *Z. mays* is taken.

Neuralgia: Liquid from the squeezed leaves of *Artemisia* spp. is taken; a decoction of equal parts *Artemisia* spp., *P. asiatica*, and *Pinus* spp. leaves is taken; liquid from the dried leaves of *Limonium* spp. soaked in liquor (*shouchuu*) is taken.

Otorrhea: Liquid from the squeezed leaves of *S. stolonifera* is poured into the ear.

Skin diseases, ringworm, scabies, etc.: The smoke from the burned leaves of *Cryptomeria japonica* is applied to the area infected with ringworm; a decoction of the leaves of *Cryptomeria japonica* is taken; a powder made from the dried fruits of *G. jasminoides* is applied to chapped hands; a decoction of the whole plant of *Kadsura japonica* is applied to chapped hands; the grated roots of *Rumex japonicus* are mixed with vinegar and applied to the area infected with ringworm.

Sprains/fractures/bruises: The grated bulbs of *C. asiaticum* are applied to the sprain; a decoction of the bark of *Elaeagnus* spp. is taken for bruises; the toasted leaves of *F. japonicum* are applied directly to the bruise; a decoction of the dried bark of *Ficus superba* is taken for bruises; the grated bulbs of

Narcissus spp. are applied to the sprain.

Stomachaches/gastrointestinal disorders: Liquid from the squeezed plant portion of *A. arborescens* is taken; a decoction of the roots of *C. zedoaria* is taken; a decoction of fresh *Pinus* spp. leaves is taken.

Swollen parts and boils: The toasted leaves of *Artemisia* spp. are applied; the young leaves of *C. camphora* are boiled in water used to wash rice, and the liquid is applied to swollen area; the toasted and squeezed leaves of *H. cordata* are applied; the squeezed leaves of *I. balsamina* are applied; the salted flowers of *I. balsamina* are applied to the throat for swollen tonsils; a decoction of the whole plant of *L. japonica* or a fully charred plant is applied; the toasted and squeezed leaves of *P. asiatica* are applied.

Tooth disease: The squeezed plant portion of *A. arborescens* is applied to the decayed tooth; the squeezed young leaves of *Morus* spp. are mixed with salt and applied to the decayed tooth.

Toxicosis: A decoction of the dried plant portion of *H. cordata* is taken.

Vermifuge: A decoction of the dried plant portion of *D. simplex* is taken.

Warts: Sap from the plant portion of *F. superba* is applied; a calyx of *S. melongena* is rubbed on the affected area.

Wounds: The squeezed plant portion of *A. arborescens* is applied; the charred bark of *C. revoluta* is kneaded with cooked rice and applied to the injured area (when you step on a nail); the toasted leaves of *F. japonicum* are applied; the squeezed leaves of *I. balsamina* are applied.

3.6. Hirano

Antipyretic: Liquid from the squeezed leaves of *Artemisia* spp. is taken; a decoction of the dried plant portion of *G. thunbergii* is taken.

Asthma: A decoction of the dried leaves and stems of *P. asiatica* is taken.

Burns: Liquid from the leaves of *A. arborescens* is applied.

Common cold: A decoction of *G. thunbergii* is taken.

Constipation: A decoction of the dried plant portion of *H. cordata* is taken.

Cough medicine or medicine promoting expectoration: A decoction of the dried leaves and stems of *P. asiatica* is taken.

Diarrhea: A decoction of the dried roots and stems of *F. japonicum* is taken; a decoction of the dried plant portion of *G. thunbergii* is taken.

Diphtheria: The grated bulbs of *A. sativum* are eaten.

Diuretic: A decoction of the dried plant portion of *H. cordata* is taken; a decoction of the dried male inflorescence of *Z. mays* is taken.

Fatigue recovery: The toasted leaves and stems of *A. sativum* are eaten.

Hemostasis: The squeezed leaves of *Artemisia* spp. are applied; *H. sibthorpioides* is applied.

Otorrhea: Liquid from the squeezed leaves of *S. stolonifera* is poured into the ear.

Skin diseases, ringworm, scabies, etc.: Liquid of the leaves of *A. arborescens* is applied to chapped hands; the dried and pounded leaves of *C. sinensis* are applied to area infected with ringworm.

Sprains/fractures/bruises: *C. zedoaria* is used for sprains and bruises (no detailed method of use is provided); the toasted leaves of *F. japonicum* are applied to the bruised area.

Stomachaches/gastrointestinal disorders: The sliced or grated plant portion of *A. arborescens* is eaten; liquid from the squeezed leaves of *Artemisia* spp. is taken; a powder made from the roots of *C. zedoaria* is taken with water; a decoction of the dried roots and stems of *F. japonicum* is taken.

Swollen parts and boils: The toasted leaves of *F. japonicum* are applied; the toasted leaves of *H. cordata* are applied; the toasted leaves of *L. maculatum* are applied; the toasted leaves of *P. asiatica* are applied.

Tooth disease: Liquid from the leaves of *A. arborescens* is applied to the decayed tooth.

Toxicosis: Resin from *Pinus* spp. (no detailed method of use is provided); the ground leaves of *S. melongena* are mixed with brown sugar and are taken for food poisoning.

Vermifuge: A decoction of the dried plant portion of *D. simplex* is taken.

Warts: A calyx of *S. melongena* is rubbed on the affected area.

Wounds: The squeezed plant portion of *Artemisia* spp. is applied; the toasted leaves of *L. maculatum* are applied.

3.7. Takabira

Bites by poisonous snakes (*mamushi*), bees, centipedes, etc.: Liquid from the stems of *C. esculenta* is applied to the insect bite.

Common cold: A decoction of *P. asiatica* is taken.

Eye injury/disease: Sap from the stems of *Vitis* spp. is used as eye drops.

Hemostasis: The squeezed leaves of *Artemisia* spp. are applied.

Skin diseases, ringworm, scabies, etc.: The fruits of *G. jasminoides* are applied to chapped hands.

Sprains/fractures/bruises: A mixture of the fruits of *G. jasminoides*, eggs, and vinegar is applied to the bruised area.

Stomachaches/gastrointestinal disorders: A decoction of the dried plant portion of *G. thunbergii* is taken; liquid from *P. mume* fruits soaked in sea water is taken; a decoction of *S. japonica* is taken.

Swollen parts and boils: *F. japonicum* (no detailed method of use is provided); the steamed leaves of *H. cordata* are applied.

Wounds: *F. japonicum* (no detailed method of use is provided).

3.8. Mugio

Antipyretic: The grated fruits of *Cucurbita* spp. are applied to the soles of the feet; the grated bulbs of *L. radiata* are applied to the soles of the feet.

Bites by poisonous snakes (*mamushi*), bees, centipedes, etc.: Liquid from the stems of *C. esculenta* is applied to the insect bite; the squeezed leaves of *Ipomoea nil* are applied to the insect bite.

Burns: Liquid from *A. arborescens* is applied; the grated tubers of *S. tuberosum* are applied.

Cancer: A decoction of the dried leaves, stems, and roots of *P. owatarii* is taken.

Constipation: A decoction of the dried roots of *Taraxacum* spp. is taken.

Diabetes: *Basella alba* leaves are eaten; a decoction of the dried leaves of *Psidium* spp. is taken.

Diarrhea: A decoction of the dried plant portion of *P. asiatica* is taken.

Eye injury/disease: Sap from the stems of *Vitis* spp. is used as eye drops.

Hemostasis: The squeezed leaves of *Artemisia* spp. are applied; the squeezed leaves of *H. sibthorpioides* are applied.

Hypertension: A decoction of the dried leaves of *D. kaki* is taken; a decoction of the dried leaves of *E. japonica* is taken; a decoction of the dried plant portion of *G. pentaphyllum* is taken; a decoction of the dried leaves of *Psidium* spp. is taken.

Kidney disease: A decoction of the dried male inflorescence of *Z. mays* is taken.

Sprains/fractures/bruises: A mixture of the fruits of *G. jasminoides*, an egg white, and wheat flour is applied to the bruised area.

Stomachaches/gastrointestinal disorders: A powder made from the dried roots of *C. zedoaria* is taken with water or a decoction of its shredded fresh roots is taken; a decoction of the dried plant portion of *G. thunbergii* is taken.

Swollen parts and boils: The toasted leaves of *F. japonicum* are applied; the squeezed leaves of *H. cordata* are applied.

Toxicosis: A decoction of the dried plant portion of *H. cordata* is taken; the salted fruits of *P. mume* dissolved in hot water are taken to remedy food poisoning.

Vermifuge: A decoction of the dried plant portion of *D. simplex* is taken.

Wounds: The charred bark of *C. revoluta* kneaded with cooked rice is applied to the injured area (when you step on a nail); the squeezed leaves and flowers of *I. balsamina* are applied.

3.9. Hara

Common cold: Rice porridge made with the leaves of *A. tuberosum* is eaten; fruit juice from *Citrus aurantium* mixed with liquor (*shouchuu*) is taken; fruit juice from *C.*

aurantium is boiled together with the leaves of *Allium fistulosum* and taken.

Diabetes: A decoction of the dried leaves of *Psidium* spp. is taken.

Diarrhea: A decoction of the dried roots of *C. zedoaria* is taken; liquid from *P. mume* fruits soaked in seawater is taken.

Eye injury/disease: Sap from the bulbs of *A. tuberosum* is used as eye drops; sap from the stems of *Vitis* spp. is used as eye drops.

Heartburn: Liquid from the squeezed leaves of *Artemisia* spp. is taken; the fresh stems of *F. japonicum* are chewed; a vine of *Paederia foetida* is wrapped around the neck.

Hemostasis: The squeezed leaves of *Artemisia* spp. are applied; the leaves of *H. sibthorpioides* are applied; the dried leaves of *Nicotiana* spp. are applied.

Hypertension: A decoction of the dried leaves (or the sour type of fruit) of *D. kaki* is taken.

Nasal congestion: A piece of the stem of *A. fistulosum* is applied to the nose.

Neuralgia: A decoction of the dried leaves of *E. japonica* is taken.

Skin diseases, ringworm, scabies, etc.: The smoke from the burned leaves of *Cryptomeria japonica* is applied to the area infected with ringworm; sap from the stems of *L. cylindrica* is applied to chapped hands.

Sprains/fractures/bruises: A decoction of the bark of *F. superba* is taken for bruises; a decoction of *Lagenaria siceraria* (no details on the particular plant parts) is taken for bruises; the steamed leaves of *Musa* spp. are applied to the bruised area; the steamed leaves of *P. asiatica* are applied to the bruised area.

Stomachaches/gastrointestinal disorders: Rice porridge made with the leaves of *A. tuberosum* is eaten; a decoction of the dried plant portion of *G. thunbergii* is taken.

Swollen parts and boils: The toasted leaves of *F. japonicum* are applied; the leaves of *H. cordata* are applied; the leaves of *P. asiatica* are applied.

Toxicosis: A decoction of the dried plant portion of *H. cordata* is taken; a decoction of *Smilax* spp. is taken.

Vermifuge: The ground fresh leaves of *Artemisia* spp. dissolved in water are taken.

Warts: The squeezed leaves of *Artemisia* spp. are applied to the affected area.

Wounds: The squeezed leaves of *Artemisia* spp. are applied; the squeezed leaves of *Centella asiatica* are applied; the squeezed flowers of *I. balsamina* are applied; the charred fresh leaves of *Morella rubra* are kneaded with cooked rice and applied.

3.10. Onoaida

Constipation: A decoction of the dried plant portion of *G. thunbergii* is taken.

Cough medicine and medicine promoting expectoration: A decoction of the dried plant portion of *P. asiatica* is taken.

Diarrhea: A decoction of the dried plant portion of *G. thunbergii* is taken.

Heartburn: The fresh stems of *F. japonicum* are chewed.

Hemostasis: The squeezed leaves of *Artemisia* spp. are applied; the inner bark of *Pinus* spp. is applied.

Hypertension: A decoction of the dried leaves of *D. kaki* is taken.

Kidney disease: A decoction of the dried roots of *Cirsium* spp. is taken; a decoction of the dried male inflorescence of *Z. mays* is taken.

Otorrhea: Liquid from the squeezed leaves of *S. stolonifera* is poured into the ear.

Stomachaches/gastrointestinal disorders: A decoction of the dried roots of *C. zedoaria* is taken; a decoction of the dried plant portion of *G. thunbergii* is taken.

Swollen parts and boils: The toasted leaves of *F. japonicum* and charred shrimp shells are kneaded with cooked rice and applied; the toasted leaves of *H. cordata* are applied; the toasted and squeezed leaves of *P. asiatica* are applied; the peel of the salted fruits of *P. mume* are applied.

Toxicosis: A decoction of the dried plant portion of *H. cordata* is taken.

3.11. Koshima

Bites by poisonous snakes (*mamushi*), bees,

centipedes, etc.: Liquid from *A. arborescens* is applied to the insect bite.

Burns: Liquid from *A. arborescens* is applied.

Common cold: A decoction of the dried plant portion of *P. asiatica* is taken.

Eye injury/disease: Sap from the stems of *Vitis* spp. is used as eye drops.

Hemostasis: The squeezed leaves of *Artemisia* spp. are applied.

Hypertension: A decoction of the dried leaves of *D. kaki* is taken.

Skin diseases, ringworm, scabies, etc.: The grated roots of *Glehnia littoralis* are applied to the area affected by scabies; the grated roots of *R. japonicus* are applied to the area infected with ringworm.

Stomachaches/gastrointestinal disorders: Liquid from *A. arborescens* is taken; a powder made from the dried roots of *C. zedoaria* is taken or a decoction of its dried roots is taken; a decoction of dried *G. thunbergii* is taken; a decoction of the roasted seeds of *Senna occidentalis* is taken.

Swollen parts and boils: The grated fresh roots of *C. zedoaria* are applied; the toasted and squeezed leaves of *F. japonicum* are applied; the toasted leaves of *H. cordata* are applied; *P. asiatica* (no detailed method of use is provided).

Tooth disease: The smoke from the burned seeds of *A. tuberosum* are held in the mouth.

Toxicosis: The cooked stems of *F. japonicum* are eaten.

Vermifuge: Liquid from the ground fresh leaves of *Artemisia* spp. is taken; a decoction of the dried plant portion of *D. simplex* is taken before every breakfast; a decoction of the dried plant portion of *H. cordata* is taken.

Wounds: Flour made from *F. esculentum* is kneaded with water and applied to the injured area (when you step on bamboo).

3.12. Hirauchi

Accidental ingestion: Liquid from the squeezed leaves and flowers of *I. balsamina* is taken to help dislodge a fishbone stuck in the throat.

Burns: The grated tubers of *S. tuberosum* are applied.

Common cold: Liquid from the finely chopped stems and leaves of *A. fistulosum* dissolved in hot water is taken; liquid from the dried flowers of *Carthamus tinctorius* dissolved in hot water is taken; fruit juice from *C. aurantium* is taken; fruit juice from *C. natsudaidai* is taken; a decoction of the fruits (or the leaves if no fruits are available) of *Fortunella* spp. is taken; a decoction of the dried plants portion (or leaves) of *P. asiatica* is taken; a powder made from the dried seeds of *Trichosanthes* spp. is taken; liquid from the grated roots of *Z. officinale* is taken.

Constipation: Liquid from the plant portion of *A. arborescens* soaked in liquor (*shouchuu*) is taken; the grated fresh plant portion of *A. arborescens* is dissolved in hot water and taken; a decoction of the dried plant portion of *A. arborescens* is taken; a decoction of the dried plant portion of *H. cordata* is taken.

Cough medicine and medicine promoting expectoration: A decoction of the fruits (or the leaves if no fruits are available) of *Fortunella* spp. is taken; *Nandina domestica* (no detailed method of use is provided).

Diabetes: A decoction of the dried roots of *C. lacryma-jobi* is taken; a decoction of the dried leaves of *Psidium* spp. is taken; a decoction of *Smilax* spp. is taken.

Diarrhea: A decoction of the dried plant portion of *G. thunbergii* is taken.

Diuretic: The fruits of *C. lanatus* are eaten.

Eye injury/disease: Liquid from the squeezed fruits of *N. domestica* is used as drops for inflamed eyes; sap from the stems of *Vitis* spp. is used for inflamed eyes.

Frostbite: The frostbitten area is soaked in hot water mixed with the leaves (or sliced roots if no leaves are available) of *Z. officinale*.

Heartburn: The fresh stems of *F. japonicum* are chewed.

Hemorrhoids: The toasted and squeezed leaves of *F. japonicum* are applied.

Hemostasis: The squeezed leaves of *Artemisia* spp. are applied.

Hypertension: A decoction of the dried leaves of *D. kaki* is taken; a decoction of the dried plant

portion of *H. cordata* is taken; a decoction of the dried leaves of *L. chinense* is taken.
Kidney disease: A decoction of the dried male inflorescence or the dried seeds of *Z. mays* is taken.
Neuralgia: A decoction of the dried leaves of *Artemisia* spp. is taken.
Otorrhea: Liquid from the squeezed leaves of *S. stolonifera* is poured into the ear.
Skin diseases, ringworm, scabies, etc.: The squeezed leaves of *C. trichotomum* are rubbed on the affected area; the toasted and squeezed leaves of *F. japonicum* are applied to rashes caused by grass; the fruits of *G. jasminoides* are used for chapped hands; a decoction of the dried plant portion of *H. cordata* is taken or its toasted and squeezed leaves are applied to rashes caused by grass; the fruits of *M. azedarach* are used for chapped hands; a mixture made of the stems of *P. foetida*, the roots of *R. japonicus*, vinegar, and sulfur is applied; liquid from the pounded roots of *R. japonicus* is mixed with vinegar and applied to the area infected with ringworm.
Sprains/fractures/bruises: A mixture made of the fruits of *G. jasminoides*, eggs, vinegar, liquor (*shouchuu*), etc. is applied to a fracture or sprain; a decoction of *L. siceraria* (no detailed plant parts) is taken for sprains or bruises.
Stomachaches/gastrointestinal disorders: A powder made from the dried roots of *C. zedoaria* is taken with water or a decoction of its dried roots is taken; a decoction of the dried plant portion of *G. thunbergii* is taken; a decoction of the roasted seeds of *S. occidentalis* is taken; moxibustion is performed using the grated roots of *Z. officinale*.
Swollen parts and boils: The charred leaves of *Camellia japonica* are kneaded with cooked rice and applied; the grated bulbs of *Crocus* spp. are applied; the toasted and squeezed leaves of *F. japonicum* are applied; the toasted and squeezed leaves of *H. cordata* are applied.
Toxicosis: A decoction of the dried plant portion of *H. cordata* is taken.
Vermifuge: A decoction of the dried plant portion of *D. simplex* (sometimes mixed with the seeds of *Cucurbita* spp.) is taken.
Warts: Sap from the bark of *F. superba* is applied; a fruit of *S. melongena* is cut in half and rubbed over the affected area.
Wounds: The squeezed leaves of *Artemisia* spp. are applied.

3.13. Yudomari

Beriberi: Liquid from the grated fresh bulbs of *Allium cepa* is taken; a decoction of the dried leaves of *P. frutescens* is taken.
Bites by poisonous snakes (*mamushi*), bees, centipedes, etc.: *A. arborescens* (no detailed method of use is provided); liquid from the stems of *C. esculenta* is applied to the bee sting; liquid from the stems of *F. japonicum* is applied to the bee sting.
Cancer: *A. elata* (no detailed method of use is provided).
Cough medicine and medicine promoting expectoration: A decoction of the dried seeds and/or the leaves and roots of *P. asiatica* is taken.
Diarrhea: A decoction of the dried plant portion of *G. thunbergii* is taken.
Diuretic: A decoction of the dried plant portion of *G. pentaphyllum* is taken.
Gynecopathy: A decoction of the dried leaves and seeds of *P. asiatica* is taken.
Hemostasis: The squeezed leaves of *Artemisia* spp. are applied.
Hypertension: *A. arborescens* (no detailed method of use is provided); a decoction of *Artemisia* spp. is taken; fruit juice from *C. unshiu* is taken; a decoction of the dried leaves of *D. kaki* is taken; a decoction of the dried plant portion of *G. pentaphyllum* is taken; a decoction of the dried fruits and leaves of *L. chinense* is taken; a decoction of the dried leaves and seeds of *P. asiatica* is taken.
Incontinence: Liquid from the squeezed plant portion of *Bidens frondosa* is taken.
Kidney disease: A decoction of the dried leaves of *E. japonica* is taken.
Neuralgia: Liquid from the grated fresh bulbs of *A. cepa* is taken.
Otorrhea: *A. arborescens* (no detailed method of

use is provided).

Rheumatism: Liquid from the grated fresh bulbs of *A. cepa* is taken.

Sprains/fractures/bruises: A decoction of *L. siceraria* (no detailed plant parts are provided) is taken to heal bruises; a decoction of the bark of *Ligustrum obtusifolium* is taken to heal bruises.

Stomachaches/gastrointestinal disorders: *A. arborescens* (no detailed method of use is provided); *C. zedoaria* (no detailed method of use is provided); a decoction of the dried plant portion of *G. thunbergii* is taken.

Swollen parts and boils: The toasted and squeezed leaves of *C. asiaticum* are applied; the toasted and squeezed leaves of *F. japonicum* are applied; the toasted and squeezed leaves of *H. cordata* are applied.

Toxicosis: A decoction of the dried plant portion of *H. cordata* is taken; a decoction of the bark of *L. obtusifolium* is taken.

Vermifuge: A decoction of the dried plant portion of *D. simplex* is taken.

Warts: Sap from the plant portion of *Ficus microcarpa* is applied; sap from the plant portion of *F. superba* is applied.

Wounds: The squeezed leaves of *Camellia japonica* are applied; flour made from *F. esculentum* is kneaded with water and applied to the injured area (when you step on bamboo); the squeezed leaves and flowers of *I. balsamina* are applied.

3.14. Nakama

Cough medicine and medicine promoting expectoration: Liquid from the boiled plant portion of *P. asiatica* is taken.

Eye injury/disease: Sap from the stems of *Vitis* spp. is used as eye drops.

Hemostatic: *Fallopia japonica* (no detailed method of use is provided).

Otorrhea: Liquid from the squeezed leaves of *S. stolonifera* is poured into the ear.

Stomachaches/gastrointestinal disorders: A decoction of the dried plant portion of *G. thunbergii* is taken.

Swollen parts and boils: The charred leaves of *Camellia japonica* are kneaded with cooked rice and applied; the toasted leaves of *F. japonicum* are applied; the toasted leaves of *H. cordata* are applied; the charred bark of *L. obtusifolium* is kneaded with cooked rice and applied; the toasted leaves of *P. asiatica* are applied.

Toxicosis: A decoction of the leaves of *N. domestica* is taken as a remedy for food poisoning.

Wounds: The squeezed leaves of *Artemisia* spp. are applied; the charred stems of *C. revoluta* are kneaded with cooked rice and applied to the injured area (when you step on a nail); the charred flour of *F. esculentum* is kneaded with cooked rice and applied to the injured area (when you step on bamboo); the squeezed leaves of *I. balsamina* are applied.

3.15. Kurio

Accidental ingestion: The grated seeds or roots of *I. balsamina* are taken to help dislodge a fishbone stuck in the throat.

Antipyretic: A decoction of the dried roots of *C. zedoaria* is taken.

Common cold: A decoction of the dried flowers of *C. tinctorius* is taken; a decoction of the dried plant portion of *P. asiatica* is taken.

Constipation: A decoction of the dried leaves and stems of *H. cordata* is taken.

Cough medicine and medicine promoting expectoration: A decoction of the dried plant portion of *P. asiatica* is taken; a decoction of the fruits of *Smilax* spp. is taken with sugar.

Diarrhea: A decoction of the dried roots and stems of *F. japonicum* is taken; a decoction of the dried plant portion of *G. thunbergii* is taken.

Diuretic: A decoction of the dried leaves and stems of *H. cordata* is taken.

Eye injury/disease: Sap from the stems of *Vitis* spp. is used as eye drops.

Gynecopathy: A decoction of the dried flowers of *C. tinctorius* is taken.

Heart disease: A decoction of the dried plant portion of *P. asiatica* is taken.

Hemostatic: The squeezed leaves of *Artemisia* spp. are applied; the squeezed leaves of *I. balsamina* are applied.

Hypertension: A decoction of the dried plant

portion of *G. thunbergii* is taken; a decoction of the dried leaves and stems of *H. cordata* is taken.

Neuralgia: The toasted and squeezed leaves of *F. japonicum* are applied; the crumpled plant portion of *Juncus effuses* is mixed with vinegar and applied to the diseased area.

Otorrhea: Liquid from the squeezed leaves of *H. cordata* is poured into the ear or the liquid is taken.

Sprains/fractures/bruises: The toasted and squeezed leaves of *F. japonicum* are applied to the bruised area; the grated roots of *R. sativus* are applied to the sprain.

Stomachaches/gastrointestinal disorders: Liquid from the squeezed leaves of *Artemisia* spp. is taken; a decoction of the dried roots of *C. zedoaria* is taken; a decoction of the dried roots and stems of *F. japonicum* is taken; a decoction of the dried plant portion of *G. thunbergii* is taken; a decoction of the dried leaves and stems of *H. cordata* is taken; a decoction of the dried bark of *Quercus dentate* is taken; a decoction of the dried plant portion of *Tetragonia tetragonoides* is taken.

Swollen parts and boils: The toasted and squeezed leaves of *F. japonicum* are applied; the toasted leaves of *H. cordata* are applied; the toasted leaves of *P. asiatica* are applied.

Vermifuge: A decoction of the dried plant portion of *D. simplex* is taken.

Wounds: The squeezed leaves of *Artemisia* spp. are applied; the charred leaves of *Camellia japonica* are kneaded with sticky rice flour and applied; the toasted and squeezed leaves of *F. japonicum* are applied; the squeezed leaves and flowers of *I. balsamina* are applied; the dried leaves of *Nicotiana* spp. are applied.

4. Characteristics of the medicinal plants in Tanega-shima and Yaku-shima islands

In Tanega-shima and Yaku-shima islands, 102 species belonging 54 families of Spermatophyta and 1 species belonging to Rhodophyceae are used as medicinal plants (Appendix 1 and 2).

Among these 102 species of Spermatophyta, more than 80% of them are native to the Old World. Of plants native to the New World, people tend to use well-known domesticated plants, such as pumpkins (*Cucurbita* spp.), sweet potatoes (*I. batatas*), tobacco (*Nicotiana* spp.), guavas (*Psidium* spp.), potatoes (*S. tuberosum*), and corn (*Z. mays*). It is suggested that people in Tanega-shima and Yaku-shima islands tend to use cultivated and wild plants native to the Old World as medicine, which is similar to the experience of Tokuno-shima Island, the Amami Islands (Yamamoto 2016).

Of the 103 species, five are recorded at almost all of the sites, used as medical plants, and applied to many diseases; *Artemisia* spp. (18 sites, for 13 diseases), *G. thunbergii* (18 sites, for 7 diseases), *F. japonicum* (17 sites, for 13 diseases), *H. cordata* (17 sites, for 14 diseases), and *P. asiatica* (17 sites, for 15 diseases). These five plants are well known as herbal medicines in Japanese Herbalism developed during the Edo Period, which may influence the popularity of these remedies. However, *G. thunbergii* and *H. cordata* are not used as medicines on Tokuno-shima Island (Yamamoto 2016), or the Ryukyu Islands (Maeda and Nose 1989) probably because *G. thunbergii* is more likely to grow in temperate zones. One missing link is the medicinal usage of *H. cordata*, which is also used as medicine in Southeast Asia (e.g., Cambodia; Kham [2004]). The reason for this missing information is unclear.

In addition to the five species noted above, 10 species are similarly popular as medicinal ingredients in Tanega-shima and Yaku-shima islands. These plants are classified into two types: those applied to many diseases or those applied to a specific disease. Plants belonging to the former type include: *C. zedoaria* (14 sites, for 6 diseases), *D. kaki* (11 sites, for 6 diseases), *A. arborescens* (10 sites, for 12 diseases), *I. balsamina* (9 sites, for 4 diseases), and *A. tuberosum* (7 sites, for 7 diseases). Plants belonging to the latter type include: *Vitis* spp. (could be *V. coignetia*e and/or *V. ficifolia*) (14 sites, for eye injury/disease), *D. simplex* (10 sites, for vermifuge), *H. sibthorpioides* (8 sites, for hemostatic), *S. stolonifera* (8 sites, mainly for otorrhea), and *Z. mays* (8 sites, for diuretic or kidney disease).

Among these 10 species, *A. arborescens*, *A. tuberosum*, *D. simplex*, and *H. sibthorpioides* are used in the same way and *Z. mays* is used differently on Tokuno-shima Island and in the Ryukyu Islands. Furthermore, *I. balsamina*, *Vitis* spp., and *S. stolonifera* are used in the same way in the Ryukyu Islands. However, *C. zedoaria* and *D. kaki* are not used for medicinal purposes in these regions. *Curcuma zedoaria* is popular as a special product in Tanega-shima and Yaku-shima islands; therefore, the population is very familiar with the use of *C. zedoaria* as a medicine. *Diospyros kaki* is a popular medicinal plant on the main islands of Japan, but it is more likely to grow successfully in temperate zones, and thus the population on Tokuno-shima Island or in the Ryukyu Islands does not use it as a medicine.

Canarium album is used as a medicine only on Tanega-shima Island partly because its fruits are a specialty product on this island. Conversely, *C. esculenta* (6 sites in Yaku-shima Island, mainly for skin diseases, ringworm, scabies, etc.) and *E. japonica* (5 sites in Yaku-shima Island, for 5 diseases) are used as medicines only on Yaku-shima Island. *Canarium album* is not used as a medicine on Tokuno-shima Island and in the Ryukyu Islands either, but *C. esculenta* is used in different ways as a medicine in the two regions and *E. japonica* is used in the same way in the Ryukyu Islands.

Further detailed studies on each island within the Nansei Islands are needed to categorize or classify the regions by medicinal plant use and traditional remedies related to plants.

References

Department of Anthropology, Faculty of Law, Economics and Humanities, Kagoshima University 1984. *Masuda no Minzokushi* (増田の民俗誌 , Folklore in Masuda). Nakatane Town Museum of History and Folklore, Nakatanechou, Kagoshima. (in Japanese)

Department of Anthropology, Faculty of Law, Economics and Humanities, Kagoshima University 1989. *Yakuchou no Minzoku* II (屋久町の民俗 II, Folklore in Yaku Town Vol. 2). 290 pp., Yakuchou Kyouiku Iinkai Kyoudoshi Hensanshitsu, Yaku-shima, Kagoshima. (in Japanese)

HIROSE, Y. 1987. *Yaku-shima Mugio no Minzokushi* II (屋久島麦生の民俗誌 II, Folklore in Mugio, Yaku-shima Island Vol. 2). 66 pp., self-published, Kagoshima. (in Japanese)

KHAM, L. 2004. Medicinal Plants of Cambodia: Habitat, Chemical Constituents and Ethnobotanical Uses, 631 pp., Bendigo Scientific Press, Australia.

MAEDA, M. and NOSE, H. (eds) 1989. *Okinawa Minzoku Yakuyou Doushokubutsushi* (沖縄民俗薬用動植物誌 , Medicinal Plants and Animals in Okinawa). 244 pp., Niraisha, Okinawa. (in Japanese)

Minamitanechou Kyoudoshi Hensan Iinkai 1987. *Minamitanechou Kyoudoshi* (南種子町郷土誌 , Folklore in Minamitane Town). 1461 pp., Minamitanechou, Kagoshima. (in Japanese)

Nakatanechou Kyoudo Henshuu Iinkai 1971. *Nakatanechou Kyoudoshi* (中種子町郷土誌 , Folklore in Nakatane Town). 1078 pp., Nakatanechou, Kagoshima. (in Japanese)

Nishinoomote Hensan Iinkai 1971. *Nishinoomoteshi Hyakunenshi* (西之表市百年史 , Hundred Years History of Nishinoomote City). 528 pp., Nishinoomoteshi, Kagoshima. (in Japanese)

Yakuchou Kyoudoshi Hensan Iinkai 1993. *Yakuchou Kyoudoshi* Vol. 1 (屋久町郷土誌第一巻 , Folklore in Yaku Town Vol. 1). 1359 pp., Yakuchou Kyouiku Iinkai, Yakuchou, Kagoshima. (in Japanese)

Yakuchou Kyoudoshi Hensan Iinkai 1995. *Yakuchou Kyoudoshi* Vol. 2 (屋久町郷土誌第二巻 , Folklore in Yaku Town Vol. 2). 963 pp., Yakuchou Kyouiku Iinkai, Yakuchou, Kagoshima. (in Japanese)

Yakuchou Kyoudoshi Hensan Iinkai 2003. *Yakuchou Kyoudoshi* Vol. 3 (屋久町郷土誌第三巻 , Folklore in Yaku Town Vol. 3). 1157 pp., Yakuchou Kyouiku Iinkai, Yakuchou, Kagoshima. (in Japanese)

YAMAMOTO, S. 2016. Medicinal Plants on Tokuno-shima Island. In: KAWAI, K., TERADA, R. and KUWAHARA, S. (eds.), The Amami Islands, Culture, Society, Industry and Nature, pp. 22–29. Hokuto Shobo Publishing, Tokyo.

Appendix 1. Abbreviations in Appendix 2.

Location		Disease name	
Abbreviation	Meaning	Abbreviation	Meaning
Tanega-shima Island	1 Nishinoomote City	Ac	Accidental ingestion
	2 Nakatane Town	An	Antipyretic
	3 Minamitane Town	As	Asthma
		Be	Beriberi
Yaku-shima Island	1 Nagakubo	Bi	Bites by poisonous snakes (*mamushi*), bees, centipedes, etc.
	2 Funayuki	Bu	Burns
	3 Matsumine	Ca	Cancer
	4 Anbou	Cm	Common cold
	5 Harumaki	Cn	Constipation
	6 Hirano	Cu	Cough medicine and medicine that promotes expectoration
	7 Takabira	Cy	Cystitis
	8 Mugio	Db	Diabetes
	9 Hara	Dr	Diarrhea
	10 Onoaida	Dp	Diphtheria
	11 Koshima	Du	Diuretic
	12 Hirauchi	Em	Empyema
	13 Yudomari	Ey	Eye injury/disease
	14 Nakama	Fa	Fatigue recovery
	15 Kurio	Fi	Filariasis
		Fr	Frostbite
		G	Gynecopathy
		Hb	Heartburn
		Hd	Heart disease
		Hr	Hemorrhoids
		Hs	Hemostasis
		Hy	Hypertension
		Ic	Ichthyism
		In	Incontinence
		K	Kidney disease
		M	Myositis
		Na	Nasal congestion
		Ne	Neuralgia
		O	Otorrhea
		P	Poor blood circulation
		R	Rheumatism
		Sk	Skin diseases, ringworm, scabies, etc.
		Sp	Sprains/fractures/bruises
		St	Stomachaches/gastrointestinal disorders
		Sw	Swollen parts and boils
		Te	Tetanus
		To	Tooth disease
		Tx	Toxicosis
		U	Urticarial
		V	Vermifuge
		Wa	Warts
		Wo	Wounds

Appendix 2. Medicinal plants of Tanega-shima and Yaku-shima islands.

Plant name	Tanega-shima Island			Yaku-shima Island														
	1	2	3	1	2	3	4	5	6	7	8	9	10	11	12	13	14	15
Acorus calamus	Wo	—	—	—	—	—	—	—	—	—	—	—	—	—	—	—	—	—
Agave spp.	—	Sk	—	—	—	—	—	—	—	—	—	—	—	—	—	—	—	—
Allium cepa	—	—	—	—	—	—	—	—	—	—	—	—	—	—	—	Be Ne R	—	—
Allium chinense	—	—	—	—	—	—	—	Ac	—	—	—	—	—	—	—	—	—	—
Allium fistulosum	—	—	—	—	—	—	—	—	—	—	—	Cm Na	—	—	Cm	—	—	—
Allium sativum	—	—	—	—	—	St	Fa	—	Dp Fa	—	—	—	—	—	—	—	—	—
Allium tuberosum	—	Sw	Wo	—	—	Ac	Ac	Ey	—	—	—	Cm Ey St	—	To	—	—	—	—
Alocasia odora	—	—	—	—	—	—	Sw	—	—	—	—	—	—	—	—	—	—	—
Aloe arborescens	—	St	—	Bi	—	Bi Hs St	As Bi Bu St	Bi Bu Dr St To Wo	Bu Sk St To	—	Bu	—	—	Bi Bu St	Cn	Bi Hy O St	—	—
Aralia elata	—	—	—	—	—	—	Db St	—	—	—	—	—	—	—	—	Ca	—	—
Artemisia spp.	Cm Hs St	St Wo	St To V Wo	Wo	Hs Hy	Hs Ne St	Hs Ne O St Wo	An Hs Ne Sw	An Hs St Wo	Hs	Hs	Hb Hs V Wa Wo	Hs	Hs V	Hs Ne Wo	Hs Hy	Wo	Hs St Wo
Arundo donax	—	—	Sk	—	—	—	—	—	—	—	—	—	—	—	—	—	—	—
Basella alba	—	—	—	—	—	—	—	—	—	—	Db	—	—	—	—	—	—	—
Bidens frondosa	—	—	—	—	—	—	—	—	—	—	—	—	—	—	—	In	—	—
Buxus microphylla	—	Fi	—	—	—	—	—	—	—	—	—	—	—	—	—	In	—	—
Camellia japonica	—	—	—	—	—	—	—	—	—	—	—	—	—	—	Sw	Wo	Sw	Wo
Camellia sinensis	—	—	Ey Sk	—	—	Sk	—	Sk	—	—	—	—	—	—	—	—	—	—
Canarium album	U	Tx	Tx	—	—	—	—	—	—	—	—	—	—	—	—	—	—	—
Carthamus tinctorius	—	—	—	—	—	—	—	—	—	—	—	—	—	—	Cm	—	—	Cm G
Centella asiatica	—	—	—	—	—	—	—	—	—	—	—	Wo	—	—	—	—	—	—
Cinnamomum camphora	—	—	Cm	—	—	—	—	Sw	—	—	—	—	—	—	—	—	—	—
Cirsium spp.	—	K	St	Ne	—	—	—	—	—	—	—	—	—	K	—	—	—	—
Citrullus lanatus	—	—	—	—	—	—	Du K	Du	—	—	—	—	—	—	Du	—	—	—
Citrus aurantium	—	—	—	—	—	—	—	—	—	—	—	Cm	—	—	Cm	—	—	—
Citrus natsudaidai	—	—	Cm Cu	—	—	—	—	—	—	—	—	—	—	—	Cm	—	—	—
Citrus unshiu	Cm	—	—	—	—	—	—	Cm	—	—	—	—	—	—	—	Hy	—	—

Appendix 2 (Continued).

Plant name	Tanega-shima Island			Yaku-shima Island														
	1	2	3	1	2	3	4	5	6	7	8	9	10	11	12	13	14	15
Clerodendrum trichotomum	—	St	Dr	—	—	—	—	—	—	—	—	—	—	—	Sk	—	—	—
Coix lacryma-jobi	—	Wa	—	—	—	—	—	—	—	—	—	—	—	—	Db	—	—	—
Colocasia esculenta	—	—	—	—	—	Bi	Bi Sp	Bi	—	Bi	Bi	—	—	—	—	Bi	—	—
Crinum asiaticum	Sw	—	—	—	—	—	Sw	Sp	—	—	—	—	—	—	—	Sw	—	—
Crocosmia x *crocosmiiflora*	—	—	—	—	—	—	—	Ca	—	—	—	—	—	—	—	—	—	—
Crocus spp.	—	—	—	—	—	—	—	—	—	—	—	—	—	—	Sw	—	—	—
Cryptomeria japonica	—	—	Bi Wo	—	—	—	—	Sk	—	—	—	Sk	—	—	—	—	—	—
Cucurbita spp.	—	—	Bi	—	—	—	—	—	—	—	An	—	—	—	V	—	—	—
Curcuma zedoaria	St	St	St	—	St	—	Hb St	St	Sp St	—	St	Dr	St	St Sw	St	St	—	An St
Cycas revoluta	Wo	Wo	—	—	—	—	Wo	Wo	—	—	Wo	—	—	—	—	—	Wo	—
Digenea simplex	—	V	V	—	—	—	V	V	V	—	V	—	—	V	V	V	—	V
Diospyros kaki	Te	—	Tx	—	—	Ne	Db G Hy	Hy	—	—	Hy	Hy	Hy	Hy	Hy	Hy	—	—
Elaeagnus spp.	Dr St	—	—	—	An	—	—	Cu Dr Sp	—	—	—	—	—	—	—	—	—	—
Eriobotrya japonica	—	—	—	—	—	—	Db Hy	G	—	—	Hy	Ne	—	—	—	K	—	—
Fagopyrum esculentum	—	—	Wo	—	—	—	—	—	—	—	—	—	Wo	—	Wo	Wo	—	—
Fallopia japonica	—	—	—	—	—	—	—	—	—	—	—	—	—	—	—	Hs	—	—
Farfugium japonicum	Ic Sw	Sw Te	St Sw Wo	—	Hb Sw	Wo	Hb Sw Tx	Hb Sp Wo	Dr Sp St Sw	Sw Wo	Sw	Hb Sw	Hb Sw	Sw Tx	Hb Hr Sk Sw	Bi Sw	Sw	Dr Ne Sp St Sw Wo
Ficus microcarpa	—	—	—	—	—	—	—	—	—	—	—	—	—	—	—	Wa	—	—
Ficus superba	—	—	—	—	—	—	—	Sp Wa	—	—	—	Sp	—	—	Wa	Wa	—	—
Fortunella spp.	—	Cu	—	—	—	—	—	—	—	—	—	—	—	—	Cm Cu	—	—	—
Gardenia jasminoides	—	Sk	—	—	—	—	—	Sk	—	Sk Sp	Sp	—	—	—	Sk Sp	—	—	—
Geranium thunbergii	St	Dr	Dr St	Dr St	Dr St	Dr St	Dr G St	Dr	An Cm Dr	St	St	St	Cn Dr St	St	Dr St	Dr St	St	Dr Hy St
Glehnia littoralis	—	—	—	—	—	—	—	—	—	—	—	—	—	Sk	—	—	—	—
Glycine max	—	—	Sk	—	—	—	—	—	—	—	—	—	—	—	—	—	—	—
Gynostemma pentaphyllum	—	—	—	—	—	Ne	Hy	—	—	—	Hy	—	—	—	—	Du Hy	—	—
Gynura bicolor	—	—	—	—	—	—	—	Hd	—	—	—	—	—	—	—	—	—	—

Appendix 2 (Continued).

Plant name	Tanega-shima Island			Yaku-shima Island														
	1	2	3	1	2	3	4	5	6	7	8	9	10	11	12	13	14	15
Houttuynia cordata	—	Fi O Sw Tx Wa	Sw Wo	Cn Em Sw	Sw Tx	St	G Sw Tx	Sw Tx	Cn Du Sw	Sw	Sw Tx	Sw Tx	Sw Tx	Sw V	Cn Hy Sk Sw Tx	Sw Tx	Sw	Cn Du Hy O St Sw
Hydrocotyle sibthorpioides	—	—	Hs	—	Hs	Hs	Hs	Hs	Hs	—	Hs	Hs	—	—	—	—	—	—
Impatiens balsamina	—	—	Wo	—	—	—	Wo	Sw Wo	—	—	Wo	Wo	—	—	Ac	Wo	Wo	Ac Hs Wo
Ipomoea batatas	—	—	Sk	—	—	—	Cn	—	—	—	—	—	—	—	—	—	—	—
Ipomoea nil	—	—	—	—	—	—	—	—	—	—	Bi	—	—	—	—	—	—	—
Juncus effusus	—	—	—	—	—	—	—	—	—	—	—	—	—	—	—	—	—	Ne
Kadsura japonica	—	—	—	—	—	—	—	Sk	—	—	—	—	—	—	—	—	—	—
Lagenaria siceraria	—	—	—	—	—	—	—	—	—	—	—	Sp	—	—	Sp	Sp	—	—
Ligustrum obtusifolium	—	—	—	—	—	—	—	—	—	—	—	—	—	—	—	Sp Tx	Sw	—
Lilium lancifolium	—	—	—	Cu	—	—	—	—	—	—	—	—	—	—	—	—	—	—
Lilium maculatum	—	—	—	—	—	—	Sw	—	Sw Wo	—	—	—	—	—	—	—	—	—
Limonium spp.	—	—	—	—	—	Ne	Ne	Ne	—	—	—	—	—	—	—	—	—	—
Lonicera japonica	—	—	Sk	—	—	—	—	Sw	—	—	—	—	—	—	—	—	—	—
Luffa cylindrica	—	—	Bi Sk	—	—	—	—	—	—	—	—	Sk	—	—	—	—	—	—
Lycium chinense	—	—	—	—	—	St	—	—	—	—	—	—	—	—	Hy	Hy	—	—
Lycoris radiata	—	—	—	—	An	—	—	—	—	—	An	—	—	—	—	—	—	—
Melia azedarach	—	V	—	V	—	—	—	—	—	—	—	—	—	—	Sk	—	—	—
Morella rubra	—	—	—	—	—	—	—	—	—	—	—	Wo	—	—	—	—	—	—
Morus spp.	Ne	—	—	—	—	—	—	To	—	—	—	—	—	—	—	—	—	—
Musa spp.	—	—	—	—	—	—	—	An	—	—	—	Sp	—	—	—	—	—	—
Nandina domestica	—	—	—	—	—	—	—	—	—	—	—	—	—	—	Cu Ey	—	Tx	—
Narcissus spp.	M	Sw	—	—	—	—	—	Sp	—	—	—	—	—	—	—	—	—	—
Nicotiana spp.	—	—	To	—	—	Hs	—	—	—	—	Hs	—	—	—	—	—	—	Wo
Oenanthe javanica	—	P	—	—	—	—	—	—	—	—	—	—	—	—	—	—	—	—
Paederia foetida	—	—	—	—	—	—	—	—	—	—	Hb	—	—	—	Sk	—	—	—
Perilla frutescens	—	—	—	—	—	—	Hy St	—	—	—	—	—	—	—	—	Be	—	—
Phytolacca spp.	—	—	—	—	—	—	Sk	—	—	—	—	—	—	—	—	—	—	—
Pinus spp.	Wo	Sk	—	—	—	—	Hb St	Ne St	—	Tx	—	—	Hs	—	—	—	—	—
Plantago asiatica	Cm	Sw	Sw	Cu Cy Ey	—	Cm Hy St	As G Hy Tx	Du Ne Sw	As Cu Sw	Cm	Dr	Sp Sw	Cu Sw	Cm Sw	Cm	Cu G Hy	Cu Sw	Cm Cu Hd Sw

Appendix 2 (Continued).

Plant name	Tanega-shima Island			Yaku-shima Island														
	1	2	3	1	2	3	4	5	6	7	8	9	10	11	12	13	14	15
Prunus mume	—	—	Dr St Tx	St	—	—	—	Cm	—	St	Tx	Dr	Sw	—	—	—	—	—
Prunus subg. *Cerasus* spp.	—	Bu	Bu	—	—	Bu	—	—	—	—	—	—	—	—	—	—	—	—
Pseudosasa owatarii	—	—	—	—	—	—	Ca Db St	Ca	—	—	Ca	—	—	—	—	—	—	—
Psidium spp.	—	—	—	—	—	—	Db Hy	—	—	—	Db Hy	Db	—	—	Db	—	—	—
Punica granatum	—	V	—	—	—	—	—	—	—	—	—	—	—	—	—	—	—	—
Quercus dentata	—	—	—	—	—	—	—	—	—	—	—	—	—	—	—	—	—	St
Raphanus sativus	—	—	—	—	—	—	Sp	—	—	—	—	—	—	—	—	—	—	Sp
Rubus sieboldii	St	—	—	—	—	—	—	—	—	—	—	—	—	—	—	—	—	—
Rumex japonicus	—	—	—	—	—	—	—	Sk	—	—	—	—	—	Sk	Sk	—	—	—
Saxifraga stolonifera	—	—	Cm	—	O	—	O	O	O	—	—	—	O	—	O	—	O	—
Senna occidentalis	—	—	—	—	—	—	—	—	—	—	—	—	—	St	St	—	—	—
Smilax spp.	—	Fi	—	—	—	—	—	—	—	—	—	Tx	—	—	Db	—	—	Cu
Solanum melongena	—	Wa	—	—	—	—	—	Wa	Tx Wa	—	—	—	—	—	Wa	—	—	—
Solanum tuberosum	—	—	—	—	—	—	—	Bu	—	—	Bu	—	—	—	Bu	—	—	—
Swertia japonica	—	St Sw	—	—	—	—	—	—	—	St	—	—	—	—	—	—	—	—
Taraxacum spp.	—	—	—	—	—	—	—	—	—	—	Cn	—	—	—	—	—	—	—
Tetragonia tetragonoides	—	—	—	—	—	—	—	—	—	—	—	—	—	—	—	—	—	St
Trichosanthes spp.	—	—	—	—	—	—	—	As	—	—	—	—	—	—	Cm	—	—	—
Vitis spp.	—	Ey	Ey	Ey	Ey	Ey	Ey	Ey	—	Ey	Ey	Ey	—	Ey	Ey	—	Ey	Ey
Zea mays	—	K	—	—	K	—	Du	K	Du	—	K	—	K	—	K	—	—	—
Zingiber mioga	—	—	—	—	Ey	—	—	—	—	—	—	—	—	—	—	—	—	—
Zingiber officinale	Cm	—	—	—	—	—	—	—	—	—	—	—	—	—	Cm Fr St	—	—	—

Urata Beach, Tanega-shima Island. Photo: Ryuta TERADA

Chapter 10
Trends in Natural Science Research on the Osumi Islands

Kei KAWAI

1. Introduction

The Amami-Ryukyu region, which includes the Osumi Islands, has fostered and maintained a high level of biodiversity as well as social and cultural diversity. In particular, this region contains locations that have been inscribed as World Natural Heritage Sites, as well as those seeking that designation, which has raised its profile internationally. Meanwhile, although future development is expected because of the region's abundant natural resources, the territorial dispute regarding the Senkaku Islands means that this is an extremely sensitive region in terms of external relations.

The Osumi Islands, which are located in the north of the Amami-Ryukyu region, include Yaku-shima, Tanega-shima, Kuro-shima, Take-shima, Iō-jima, Mage-shima, Shōwa Iō-jima, and Kuchinoerabu-jima. The region supports a rich natural environment with impressive biodiversity centered on Yaku-shima. It was inscribed as a World Natural Heritage Site in 1993, which has led to an increase in tourism in the region.

Many scholars have conducted studies of this region, but their aims and subjects have changed over the years. Many research document databases have already been compiled, and keyword searches of these databases make it possible to investigate what types of research have been conducted in each period. For this chapter, we aimed to use the repositories of major universities to reveal the keywords that have been used for the studies that have been conducted, in particular, in the area of natural science. The academic institution repositories used are shown in Fig. 1 and Table 1, and are from universities all across Japan, from Hokkaido in the north to Okinawa in the south. Thus, it is possible to investigate research trends in the various regions. Finally, the studies published in this chapter are summarized at the end for reference.

2. Methods

To identify the studies pertaining to islands that have been conducted by the research institutions listed in Table 1, we searched for the term "island" in each database to obtain a list of relevant titles. Text mining was then used to identify the 1000 most-used terms in the titles. From these, experts in the fields of medicine, terrestrial zoology, botany, marine biology, the fishing industry, and agriculture selected the terms that they considered to be the most important. In addition, we determined the number of studies on each of the seven major islands in the Osumi Islands (Yaku-

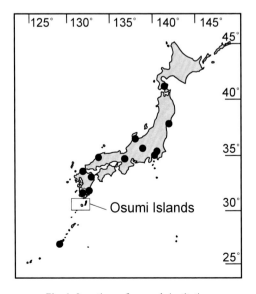

Fig. 1. Locations of research institutions managing databases used in the search (●).

Table 1. Number of papers published at each university by island.

	Yaku-shima	Tanega-shima	Mage-shima	Io-jima	Kuro-shima	Take-shima	Kuchierabu-jima	Total
Kyoto Univ	638	50	2	20	31	179	27	947
Shinshu Univ.	3	0	0	1	1	3	0	8
Shimane Univ.	1	1	0	1	0	2	0	5
Tokyo Univ. of Foreign Studies	0	0	0	0	2	0	0	2
Tohoku Univ.	0	0	0	0	0	0	0	0
Univ. Miyazaki	2	0	0	0	0	0	0	2
Future Univ. Hakodate	0	0	0	0	0	0	0	0
Kanagawa Univ.	0	0	0	3	5	13	0	21
Ritsumeikan Univ.	0	0	0	0	0	1	0	1
Kyushu Univ.	32	20	0	13	2	50	3	120
Aoyama Gakuin Univ.	0	0	0	0	0	0	0	0
Univ. Tokyo	35	18	1	16	7	13	0	90
Kagoshima Univ.	201	160	12	55	59	53	0	540
Ohita Univ.	1	1	0	0	0	0	0	2
Kanazawa Univ.	12	14	0	7	36	48	0	117
Univ. Ryukyus	14	17	0	2	77	21	2	133
Total	939	281	15	118	220	383	32	1988

shima, Tanega-shima, Iō-jima, Take-shima, Kuro-shima, Mage-shima, and Kuchinoerabu-jima) by searching for each name.

3. Results and Discussion
3.1 Research activity at each university
Table 1 shows the number of research papers from each university concerning the seven named islands. The total number of papers published regarding the seven islands combined was highest for Kyoto University at 947 results, followed by Kagoshima University, which is near the region in question, and then by the University of the Ryukyus, which neighbors the region. No significant trends were observed between the number of papers regarding individual islands and the number of educators, academic departments, or founding year for each university, as shown in Table 2. It is likely that Kyoto University ranked first in total number of island papers published because of the intensive research conducted around the Kyoto University Yaku-shima Field Station on Yaku-shima. From this, it can be understood that much of the research has been performed by local universities or universities with a base of operations in the region of interest.

The highest number of studies was conducted on Yaku-shima, followed by Take-shima, Tanega-shima, Kuro-shima, Iō-jima, Kuchinoerabu-jima, and Mage-shima (Table 1). The amount of research activity on each island is believed to be affected by its importance and diversity in terms of society, culture, and natural science, as well as the size, transportation costs, and convenience of transportation, as shown in Table 3. Yaku-shima and Tanega-shima are believed to be at the top of the study ranking for such reasons. However, in our results, Take-shima ranked above Tanega-shima, despite the former having a smaller surface area. As the name Take-shima is better known in Japan, this high search result count could be from the seven islands (Center for Research and Promotion of Japanese Islands 2004) being searched for by island name alone. The same can be said about Iō-jima and Kuro-shima, and so it is possible that there are not many studies about individual islands other than studies on Yaku-shima and Tanega-shima in the Osumi Islands.

3.2. Keywords regarding studies

As a result of investigating the text-mined keywords obtained from the published study titles, 21 keyword terms in the field of natural science were found to be important in research in this region, as shown in Table 4. Since these keywords were selected from studies originating from all across Japan, they tended toward generic to the whole country. For example, major current global issues such as globalization and sustainability are important issues in the Osumi Islands, as well as in the rest of Japan. In contrast, other important keyword terms in natural science were specific to the region, including the biodiversity of Yaku-shima, which has been inscribed as a World Natural Heritage Site (ex. YAMAGUCHI 1995); the Tanega-shima Space Center run by JAXA (ex. Appl. Meteorological Eng. and Cons. Serv. 1997); the landscape of Iō-jima, Kuro-shima, and Take-shima, which are part of the Japanese Geoparks Network (ex. FUKAMI 2014); and the volcanic activity of Iō-jima and Kuchinoerabu-jima (ex. KOBAYASHI 2016).

3.3. Studies discussed in this chapter

Six papers are published in this chapter. Hiroyuki MOTOMURA reviewed the Ichthyofauna of Yaku-shima Island. Hiroshi SUZUKI describes the relationship between volcanic fumaroles and a population of crabs belonging to the genus

Table 2. Comparative information on each university.

	Number of students	Number of stuff	Number of faculties
Kyoto Univ.	13421	1117	10
Shinshu Univ.	9264	599	8
Shimane Univ.	5410	486	5
Tokyo Univ. of Foreign Studies	3816	181	1
Tohoku Univ.	11003	1673	10
Univ. Miyazaki	4723	370	4
Future Univ. Hakodate	1073	63	1
Kanagawa Univ.	18013	416	7
Ritsumeikan Univ.	32280	1042	13
Kyushu Univ.	11791	936	11
Aoyama Gakuin Univ.	17685	438	9
Univ. Tokyo	14013	1701	10
Kagoshima Univ.	8993	582	9
Ohita Univ.	5040	315	4
Kanazawa Univ.	7969	680	3
Univ. Ryukyus	6818	557	7

Table 3. Comparative information on each of the Osumi Islands.

	Size (km^2)	Population	Number of airports	Number of seaports	Number of accomodations
Yaku-shima	504.86	13706	1	16	35
Tanega-shima	445.52	35695	1	10	32
Mage-shima	8.20	0	0	2	0
Io-jima	11.65	150	0	1	4
Kuro-shima	15.37	259	0	2	4
Take-shima	4.20	91	0	2	2
Kuchienoerabu-jima	38.04	169	0	3	6

Xenograpsus. Toshiyuki HAMADA introduces a study searching for substances derived from natural products in Kagoshima. Yūjin KITAMURA explains the structural geology research of the Shimanto Group at Tanega-shima. Yasushi OHTSUKA describes a survey of black flies of the family Simuliidae acting as a vector for filariasis in the Osumi Islands. Finally, Ryuta TERADA takes us through a survey of the distribution of seaweeds on the Osumi Islands.

References

Appl. Meteorological Eng. & Cons. Serv. 1997. Tanega-shima Space Center meteorological observation data handbook: 1975–1994 report. National Space Development Agency of Japan (NASDA), Japan.

Center for Research and Promotion of Japanese Islands. 2004. *Shimadas*. 1327 pp., Sanshusha, Tokyo. (in Japanese)

FUKAMI, F. 2014. Potential construction of a geopark in small islands: Preliminary qualitative action research on the geopark concept in the Mishima Village, Kagoshima Prefecture, Japan. Northeast Asia Tourism Research 10(1): 289–309.

KOBAYASHI, T. 2016. Volcanic islands of Kagoshima. Toushoken Booklet Vol. 3. 65 pp., Hokuto Shobo Publishing, Tokyo. (in Japanese)

YAMAGUCHI, H. 1995. Yakushima of World Natural Heritage. Pre-prints of Symposium on Global Environment, Vol 5., 243 pp.

Table 4. Natural science keywords selected as important in six fields (medicine, terrestrial zoology, botany, marine biology, the fishing industry, and agriculture)

topography	area	coral reef
ecology of plant	globalization	water temperature
vegetation	distribution	water quality
natural environment	ecology	conservation
classification	Amami	sustainable
Nansei Islands	current	growth
heavy rain	Tsunami	river

Chapter 11
Review of the Ichthyofauna of Yaku-shima Island in the Osumi Islands, Southern Japan, with 15 New Records of Marine Fishes

Hiroyuki MOTOMURA

1. Introduction

Yaku-shima Island is located ca. 60 km off south-southwest of Osumi Peninsula, Kagoshima Prefecture, southern Japan. The island, roughly circular in shape and with an area of ca. 505 km² and several mountains more than 1,000 m in height (highest 1,936 m), is the largest island in the Osumi Islands (MOTOMURA et al. 2010). Yaku-shima Island, formed mostly of granite, has very limited flatlands and in its entirety appears as one large, steep mountain, with the mountain slope continuing under the sea. Thus, shallow waters, coral reefs and sandy beaches are very limited; most coastal areas are occupied by rocky reefs. Although such a monotonous environment in the coastal areas of an oceanic island generally results in a decrease in fish species diversity, Yaku-shima Island has a relatively higher diversity because the island faces a warm, strong water current, the Kuroshio Current, which brings tropical fishes from the south (MOTOMURA et al. 2010, MOTOMURA 2012, 2015).

In this chapter, the history of ichthyofaunal studies at Yaku-shima Island and ichthyofaunal features of the island are reviewed. In addition, 15 species are herein listed as the first specimen-based records of the species from Yaku-shima Island.

2. Material and methods

Sampling methods were described and illustrated in MOTOMURA et al. (2010). Curatorial procedures for collected specimens followed MOTOMURA and ISHIKAWA (2013). Standard length is abbreviated as SL. Specimens newly collected from Yaku-shima Island have been deposited at fish collections of the Kagoshima University Museum, Kagoshima, Japan (KAUM).

3. History of ichthyofaunal studies at Yaku-shima Island

In 1904–1905, Mr. Robert ANDERSON, who was a graduate student of Stanford University and studied birds, collected fishes from Yaku-shima Island. His collection was sent to the United States National Museum and Stanford University. His fish collection is most likely to be the oldest available specimens from the island. JORDAN and STARKS (1906) reported 13 species of fishes from Yaku-shima Island on the basis of ANDERSON's collection. These specimens are currently deposited at the Museum Support Center of the Smithsonian Institution National Museum of Natural History, Suitland (formerly United States National Museum) and the California Academy of Sciences, San Francisco (all fish specimens moved from Stanford University around 1969) (MOTOMURA et al. 2010). Subsequently, ARAI and IDA (1975) reported 80 species from Kusugawa, Yaku-shima Island on the basis of collected specimens; most of their specimens were deposited at the National Museum of Nature and Science, Tsukuba.

Several reports on fishes from Yaku-shima Island (e.g. ICHIKAWA et al. 1992, KUNIYASU 1999, MATSUMOTO 2001) were published by local divers and nature guides. These were based on underwater investigations, including underwater observations, photographs and movies, and observation at local fish markets; no voucher specimens were retained. Detailed information on the reports was given in MOTOMURA et al. (2010).

MOTOMURA et al. (2010) provided a list of 951 species of marine and estuarine fishes (382 genera, 112 families, and 24 orders) occurring off Yaku-shima Island on the basis of published papers, underwater photographs, and 4,386 collected specimens, along with color photographs where available. The examined specimens have been deposited at collections of Laboratory of Marine Biology, Faculty of Science, Kochi University; Fisheries Research Laboratory, Mie University; Kagoshima University Museum; Kanagawa Prefectural Museum of Natural History; Division of Fisheries Sciences, Faculty of Agriculture, University of Miyazaki; and National Museum of Nature and Science. Yonezawa et al. (2010) listed 32 species of freshwater fishes from Yaku-shima Island.

After a comprehensive review of fishes of Yaku-shima Island by Motomura et al. (2010), Matsunuma et al. (2011), Ohashi and Motomura (2011), and Yoshida et al. (2011) recorded as first records from the island, one scorpaenid, one soleid, and five apogonids, respectively, on the basis of specimens deposited at the Coastal Branch of Natural History Museum and Institute, Chiba, Japan (CMNH). Motomura and Aizawa (2011) examined all specimens of fishes (except for Gobioidei) from Yaku-shima Island deposited at CMNH and reported additional 29 species from the island for the first time, plus further 21 species represented by voucher specimens, having been previously recorded from the island only by underwater observations and/or from photographs. Of the 50 voucher-based species newly recorded by Motomura and Aizawa (2011), 11 represented a northernmost range extension and one, a southernmost extension. Murase et al. (2011) reported one species of blennid for the first time from Yaku-shima Island. Kato (2011) published underwater photographs of two species of gobiids from Yaku-shima Island which have at no time been recorded from the island.

Between 2012 and 2016, a total of 83 species were newly recorded from Yaku-shima Island on the basis of collected specimens: 1 species of exocoetid (recorded by Hata and Motomura 2014), 1 holocentrid (Eguchi and Motomura 2016), 1 syngnathid (Tashiro and Motomura 2015), 1 sebastid (Iwatsubo et al. 2015), 1 hexagrammid (Motomura 2015), 2 serranids (Yoshida and Motomura 2014, Fujiwara et al. 2015), 2 apogonids (Yoshida and Motomura 2015a,b), 1 pempherid (Koeda et al. 2015), 1 lutjanid (Matsunuma and Motomura 2014), 4 eleotrids (Akihito et al. 2013), 1 xenisthmid (Akihito et al. 2013), 62 gobiids (Akihito et al. 2013, Murase 2015), and 4 microdesmids (Akihito et al. 2013).

4. New records from Yaku-shima Island in this study

During the recent Yaku-shima expeditions by the Kagoshima University Museum from 2011 to 2015, 544 specimens of fishes were collected from the island and registered in fish collection of the museum. From the 544 specimens, nine species were reported as the first records from the island in 2014–2016 (Hata and Motomura 2014, Matsunuma and Motomura 2014, Iwatsubo et al. 2015, Yoshida and Motomura 2015a,b, Tashiro and Motomura 2015, Fujiwara et al. 2015, Koeda et al. 2015, Eguchi and Motomura 2016; see above). Examination of the 544 specimens during this study showed that 15 species (with 27 specimens) had not been recorded from Yaku-shima Island. Thus, the 15 species are listed below as the first specimen-based records from Yaku-shima Island, with registration numbers, sizes, localities in the island, collection depths, and remarks. Color photographs of the 15 species are given in Figure 1.

The above mentioned published records and new records in this study bring the total number of marine and freshwater fish species for Yaku-shima Island to 1,138, the highest fish species diversity recorded from a single region in Japan [second greatest fish species diversity recorded from Iriomote-jima Island in the Yaeyama Islands, near Taiwan, with 1,082 species (Senou et al. 2006)].

SCORPAENIDAE

Parascorpaena mcadamsi (Fowler 1938)
[Japanese name: Togeitten-fusakasago] Fig. 1A, B
KAUM–I. 38332, 37.6 mm SL, off Nagata, 30°23′35″N, 130°23′05″E, 5 m depth, 9 June 2011; KAUM–I. 68009, 56.1 mm SL, off Isso, 30°27′45″N, 130°29′40″E, 10–15 m, 26 Dec. 2014.

Remarks: Taxonomic status of this species was discussed by MOTOMURA (2013).

Parascorpaena moultoni (WHITLEY 1961)
[Itten-fusakasago] Fig. 1C
KAUM–I. 42019, 43.6 mm SL, off Isso, 30°27′45″N, 130°29′40″E, 25 m, 22 Oct. 2011.
Remarks: This nominal species, previously treated as an unknown name, was regarded as a valid species by MOTOMURA et al. (2011). This species is currently known from Kochi, Kagoshima, and Okinawa prefectures in Japanese waters (MOTOMURA 2013).

Scorpaenopsis macrochir OGILBY 1910
[Marusube-kasago] Fig. 1D
KAUM–I. 41800, 89.5 mm SL, off Harutahama, Ambo, 30°17′56″N, 130°39′11″E, 5 m, 17 Oct. 2011.
Remarks: The present specimen represents the northernmost record for the species. It is common in sandy bottoms near and among rocky reefs off Harutahama.

CARACANTHIDAE
Caracanthus maculatus (GRAY 1831)
[Dango-okoze] Fig. 1E
KAUM–I. 68049, 26.0 mm SL, off Nagata, 30°23′35″N, 130°23′06″E, 5–10 m, 27 Dec. 2014.
Remarks: This species has frequently been treated as a member of the family Scorpaenidae. Common in coral reefs, but rarely collected.

SEBASTIDAE
Helicolenus hilgendorfii (DÖDERLEIN 1884)
[Yume-kasago] Fig. 1F
KAUM–I. 38090, 255.8 mm SL, off Yaku-shima Island (purchased at Marudaka Fishery), 7 June 2011.
Remarks: This deep water species, usually collected deeper than 100 m, is probably common off Yaku-shima Island.

PLATYCEPHALIDAE
Sunagocia otaitensis (CUVIER 1829)
[Fusakuchi-gochi] Fig. 1G
KAUM–I. 38141, 153.8 mm SL, tidepool in Kurio, 30°15′58″N, 130°24′52″E, 0–1.5 m, 8 June 2011.
Remarks: This species has been recorded from the Izu, Ogasawara, and Ryukyu islands in Japanese waters. The present specimen represents the northernmost record of the species in the Ryukyu Islands.

SERRANIDAE
Caprodon schlegelii (GÜNTHER 1859)
[Akaisaki] Fig. 1H, I
KAUM–I. 38091, 240.1 mm SL, KAUM–I. 38100, 240.1 mm SL, off Yaku-shima Island (purchased at Marudaka Fishery), 7 June 2011.
Remarks: This species is common around Yaku-shima Island.

Pseudanthias hypselosoma BLEEKER 1878
[Kerama-hanadai] Fig. 1J
KAUM–I. 38120, 38.1 mm SL, KAUM–I. 38121, 41.1 mm SL, KAUM–I. 38122, 42.5 mm SL, KAUM–I. 38123, 42.2 mm SL, KAUM–I. 38124, 42.3 mm SL, off Isso, 30°27′25″N, 130°29′31″E, 20–25 m, 8 June 2011.
Remarks: This species is common around Yaku-shima Island.

PSEUDOCHROMIDAE
Pseudoplesiops annae (WEBER 1913)
[Kamereon-tanabatamegisu] Fig. 1K
KAUM–I. 67979, 28.5 mm SL, KAUM–I. 67981, 27.7 mm SL, KAUM–I. 67988, 27.5 mm SL, KAUM–I. 67990, 38.9 mm SL, KAUM–I. 68005, 20.1 mm SL, off Isso, 30°27′45″N, 130°29′40″E, 10–15 m, 26 Dec. 2014.
Remarks: This species was reported by YOSHIDA (2013) as the first Japanese record from Iou-jima Island in the Osumi Islands. Subsequently, 13 specimens of the species were recorded by YOSHIDA et al. (2013) from Amami-oshima Island in the Amami Islands.

SCOMBROPIDAE
Scombrops boops (HOUTTUYN 1782)
[Mutsu] Fig. 1L
KAUM–I. 41802, 414.8 mm SL, off Yaku-shima Island (purchased at Marudaka Fishery), 17 Oct.

Fig. 1. Fishes newly collected from Yaku-shima Island in the Osumi Islands. A–B, *Parascorpaena mcadamsi* (A, KAUM–I. 38332, 37.6 mm SL; B, KAUM–I. 68009, 56.1 mm SL); C, *P. moultoni* (KAUM–I. 42019, 43.6 mm SL); D, *Scorpaenopsis macrochir* (KAUM–I. 41800, 89.5 mm SL); E, *Caracanthus maculatus* (KAUM–I. 68049, 26.0 mm SL); F, *Helicolenus hilgendorfii* (KAUM–I. 38090, 255.8 mm SL); G, *Sunagocia otaitensis* (KAUM–I. 38141, 153.8 mm SL); H–I, *Caprodon schlegelii* (H, KAUM–I. 38100, 240.1 mm SL; I, KAUM–I. 38091, 240.1 mm SL); J, *Pseudanthias hypselosoma* (KAUM–I. 38123, 42.2 mm SL); K, *Pseudoplesiops annae* (KAUM–I. 67979, 28.5 mm SL); L, *Scombrops boops* (KAUM–I. 41802, 414.8 mm SL); M, *Pristipomoides argyrogrammicus* (KAUM–I. 38089, 258.0 mm SL); N, *P. filamentosus* (KAUM–I. 38099, 314.7 mm SL); O, *P. sieboldii* (KAUM–I. 41803, 306.2 mm SL); P, *Plectroglyphidodon imparipennis* (KAUM–I. 38338, 41.4 mm SL); Q, *Platax boersii* (KAUM–I. 41829, 62.0 mm SL).

2011.

Remarks: This species is common around Yaku-shima Island.

LUTJANIDAE

Pristipomoides argyrogrammicus (VALENCIENNES 1832)

[Hanafuedai] Fig. 1M
KAUM–I. 38089, 258.0 mm SL, off Yaku-shima Island (purchased at Marudaka Fishery), 7 June 2011.
Remarks: This species is common around Yaku-shima Island.

Pristipomoides filamentosus (VALENCIENNES 1830)
[Ohime] Fig. 1N
KAUM–I. 38099, 314.7 mm SL, off Yaku-shima Island (purchased at Marudaka Fishery), 7 June 2011.
Remarks: This species is common around Yaku-shima Island.

Pristipomoides sieboldii (BLEEKER 1855)
[Himedai] Fig. 1O
KAUM–I. 41803, 306.2 mm SL, off Yaku-shima Island (purchased at Marudaka Fishery), 17 Oct. 2011.
Remarks: This species is common around Yaku-shima Island.

POMACENTRIDAE
Plectroglyphidodon imparipennis (VAILLANT and SAUVAGE 1875)
[Iwasaki-suzumedai] Fig. 1P
KAUM–I. 38336, 21.6 mm SL, KAUM–I. 38338, 41.4 mm SL, KAUM–I. 38339, 44.2 mm SL, off Nagata, 30°23′35″N, 130°23′05″E, 5 m, 9 June 2011.
Remarks: This species is common at coral reefs in Yaku-shima Island.

EPHIPPIDAE
Platax boersii BLEEKER 1852
[Mikaduki-tsubameuo] Fig. 1Q
KAUM–I. 41829, 62.0 mm SL, Yoshida Fishing Port, Yoshida, 30°26′12″N, 130°27′59″E, 3 m, 18 Oct. 2011.
Remarks: This species is common around Yaku-shima Island.

5. Zoogeographical implications of the Yaku-shima Island ichthyofauna

MOTOMURA et al. (2010) suggested that the fish fauna of Yaku-shima Island is more similar to that of the Ryukyu Islands, rather than that of the Pacific coast of Japan, based on analysis of the top eight speciose families of fishes in the Sagami Sea, Yaku-shima Island, Ie-jima Island, and the Miyako Group. The similarity between the fish faunas of Yaku-shima Island and the Ryukyu Islands is most likely caused by transportation of tropical fishes, such as Apogonidae and Pomacentridae, by the Kuroshio Current from Taiwan or China to Yaku-shima Island (MOTOMURA et al. 2010, MOTOMURA 2012). Subsequently, cluster analysis of fishes from 12 localities in southern Japan also showed that there were two distinctive biogeographical regions in Japanese waters: one is the Japanese mainland and the Izu and Ogasawara islands, and the other is the Ryukyu Islands, including Yaku-shima Island (MATSUURA and SENOU 2012: fig. 1.5).

MOTOMURA et al. (2010) also discovered that some temperate species, such as Parupeneus spilurus (Mullidae), that occur off the Japanese mainland (and often off Taiwan) and do not occur in the Ryukyu Islands, were well established in Yaku-shima Island. Subsequently, MOTOMURA (2015) and IWATSUBO et al. (2015) reported two temperate species (usually distributed in northern Japan) from Yaku-shima Island with a huge southward distributional range extension. These suggest that an unknown southward water current from southern Kyushu to Yaku-shima Island exists and some temperate fishes are transported by the current.

Several species are known to have speciated in the north and south of the Tokara Islands, resulting in two sister species being allopatrically distributed in the Japanese mainland with associated islands, including Yaku-shima Island (north of the Tokara Islands), and the Amami Islands and southward (south of the Tokara Islands) (MOTOMURA et al. 2010). However, in some cases, two sister species occur sympatrically at Yaku-shima Island (MOTOMURA et al. 2010, MOTOMURA 2012, 2015). This phenomenon is known only from Yaku-shima Island in Japan. The characteristics of ichthyofauna of Yaku-shima Island were discussed in detail in MOTOMURA et al. (2010) and MOTOMURA (2012, 2015).

Acknowledgments

I am grateful to Y. Haraguchi, M. Nishihara, H. Iwatsubo, T. Uejo, H. Tatsukawa, and other volunteers, and students of KAUM for their curatorial assistance, and T. Yoshida and H. Hata (KAUM) for identifying some species from Yaku-shima Island. This study was supported in part by JSPS KAKENHI Grant Numbers JP26241027, JP24370041, JP23580259, and JP26450265; the JSPS Core-to-Core Program, "Research and Education Network on Southeast Asian Coastal Ecosystems"; the "Coastal Area Capability Enhancement in Southeast Asia Project" of the Research Institute for Humanity and Nature, Kyoto, Japan; the "Biological Properties of Biodiversity Hotspots in Japan" project of the National Museum of Nature and Science, Tsukuba, Japan; and the "Establishment of Research and Education Network on Biodiversity and Its Conservation in the Satsunan Islands" project of Kagoshima University adopted by the Ministry of Education, Culture, Sports, Science and Technology, Japan.

References

Akihito, Sakamoto, K., Ikeda, Y. and Aizawa, M. 2013. Gobioidei. In: Nakabo, T. (ed.), Fishes of Japan with pictorial keys to the species, third edition, pp. 1347–1608, 2109–2211. Tokai Univ. Press, Hadano.

Arai, R. and Ida, H. 1975. The sea fishes of Yaku-shima and Tanega-shima Islands, southern Kyushu, Japan. Mem. Natl. Sci. Mus. (8): 183–204.

Eguchi, K. and Motomura, H. 2016. Holocentrid fishes of the Ryukyu Islands, Japan. Nat. Kagoshima 42: 57–112. (free PDF available at http://www.kagoshima-nature.org/)

Fujiwara, K., Takayama, M., Sakurai, Y. and Motomura, H. 2015. Records of *Epinephelus bleekeri* (Perciformes: Serranidae) from Japan, with notes on distributional implications. Taxa, Proc. Japan. Soc. Syst. Zool. 39: 40–46.

Hata, H. and Motomura, H. 2014. First record of *Cypselurus spilonotopterus* (Beloniformes: Exocoetidae) from the Kagoshima mainland, southern Japan. Nat. Kagoshima 40: 25–28. (free PDF available at http://www.kagoshima-nature.org/)

Ichikawa, S., Sunakawa, S. and Matsumoto, T. 1992. A general view of fishes of Yaku-shima Island [original title in Japanese: *Yaku-shima san gyorui no gaikan*]. In: Team for Marine Organism Survey in Inshore of Yaku-shima Island [*Yaku-shima engan kaiyou seibutsu chousadan*] (eds.), pp. 19–46. Report on Scientific Survey of Marine Organisms from Inshore of Yaku-shima Island [*Yaku-shima engan kaiyou seibutsu gakujyutsu chousa houkokusyo*].

Iwatsubo, H., Yamaguchi, M., Hata, H. and Motomura, H. 2015. Occurrence of Goldeye Rockfish, *Sebastes thompsoni* (Perciformes: Sebastidae), from Yaku-shima island in the Osumi Group, Kagoshima Prefecture, southern Japan. Nat. Kagoshima 41: 41–45. (free PDF available at http://www.kagoshima-nature.org/)

Jordan, D. S. and Starks, E. C. 1906. List of fishes collected on Tanega and Yaku, offshore islands of southern Japan, by Robert Van Vleck Anderson, with descriptions of seven new species. Proc. US Natl. Mus. 30 (1462): 695–706.

Kato, S. 2011. Marine fishes illustrated. 303 pp. Seibundo-Shinkosha, Tokyo.

Koeda, K., Kaburagi, K. and Motomura, H. 2015. Records of *Pempheris oualensis* (Perciformes: Pempheridae) from the Satsunan Islands, Ryukyu Archipelago, Japan. Bull. Biogeogr. Soc. Japan 70: 275–282.

Kuniyasu, T. (ed.). 1999. Report on regional survey of ecosystem diversity (inshore of Yaku-shima Island) [original title in Japanese: *Seitaikei tayousei chiiki chousa (Yaku-shima engan kaiiki)*]. 64 pp., Nature Conservation Bureau, Ministry of Environment and Kagoshima Nature Conservation Association [*Kankyou-chou shizenhogo-kyoku · Kagoshimaken shizenaigo-kyoukai*].

Matsumoto, T. 2001. Chaetodontid fishes in Yaku-shima Island [original title in Japanese: *Yaku-shima no chouchouuo-ka gyorui ni tsuite*]. YNAC Tsushin (12): 8–9.

Matsunuma, M., Aizawa, M., Sakurai, Y. and Motomura, H. 2011. Record of a lionfish, *Pterois mombasae*, from Yaku-shima Island, southern Japan, and notes on distributional implications of the species and *P. antennata* in Japan (Scorpaenidae). Nat. Kagoshima 37: 3–8. (free PDF available at http://www.kagoshima-nature.org/)

Matsunuma, M. and Motomura, H. 2014. Northernmost records of *Lutjanus dodecacanthoides* (Lutjanidae) from the Osumi Group, southern Japan. Taxa, Proc. Japan. Soc. Syst. Zool. 37: 14–20.

Matsuura, K. and Senou, H. 2012. The Kuroshio Current and fishes. In: Matsuura, K. (ed.), Fishes in the Kuroshio Current, pp. 3–16. Tokai Univ. Press, Tokyo.

Motomura, H. 2012. Fish diversity in Kagoshima influenced by the Kuroshio Current. In: Matsuura, K. (ed.), Fishes in the Kuroshio Current, pp. 19–45. Tokai Univ. Press, Tokyo.

Motomura, H. 2013. Scorpaenidae. In: Motomura, H., Dewa, S., Furuta, K. and Matsuura, K. (eds.), Fishes of Iou-jima and Take-shima islands, Mishima, Kagoshima, Japan, pp. 36–66. Kagoshima Univ. Mus., Kagoshima and Natl. Mus. Nat. Sci., Tsukuba. (free PDF available at http://www.museum.kagoshima-u.ac.jp/staff/motomura/dl.html)

Motomura, H. 2015. Fish species diversity in the Ryukyu Islands. In: Ecol. Soc. Japan (ed.), Biodiversity, formation history, and conservation in the Nansei Islands. Ecology lectures 8, pp. 56–63. Nanpou Shinsya, Kagoshima.

Motomura, H. and Aizawa, M. 2011. Illustrated list of

additions to the ichthyofauna of Yaku-shima Island, Kagoshima Prefecture, southern Japan: 50 new records from the island. Check List, 7: 448–457.

MOTOMURA, H., BÉAREZ, P. and CAUSSE, R. 2011. Review of Indo-Pacific specimens of the subfamily Scorpaeninae (Scorpaenidae), deposited in the Museum national d'Histoire naturelle, Paris, with description of a new species of *Neomerinthe*. Cybium 35: 55–73.

MOTOMURA, H. and ISHIKAWA, S. (eds.) 2013. Fish collection building and procedures manual. English edition. 70 pp., Kagoshima Univ. Mus., Kagoshima and Res. Inst. Humanity Nat., Kyoto. (free PDF available at http://www.museum.kagoshima-u.ac.jp/staff/motomura/dl_en.html)

MOTOMURA, H., KURIIWA, K., KATAYAMA, E., SENOU, H., OGIHARA, G., MEGURO, M., MATSUNUMA, M., TAKATA, Y., YOSHIDA, T., YAMASHITA, M., KIMURA, S., ENDO, H., MURASE, A., IWATSUKI, Y., SAKURAI, Y., HARAZAKI, S., HIDAKA, K., IZUMI, H. and MATSUURA, K. 2010. Annotated checklist of marine and estuarine fishes of Yaku-shima Island, Kagoshima, southern Japan. In: MOTOMURA, H. and MATSUURA, K. (eds.), Fishes of Yaku-shima Island – A World Heritage island in the Osumi Group, Kagoshima Prefecture, southern Japan, pp. 65–248. Natl. Mus. Nat. Sci., Tokyo. (free PDF available at http://www.museum.kagoshima-u.ac.jp/staff/motomura/dl_en.html)

MURASE, A. 2015. Ichthyofaunal diversity and vertical distribution patterns in the rockpools of the southwestern coast of Yaku-shima Island, southern Japan. Check List 11 (1682): 1–21.

MURASE, A., HARAZAKI, S., MEGURO, M. and MOTOMURA, H. 2011. Northernmost records of three blenniid fishes (Teleostei: Perciformes) from Yaku-shima Island, southern Japan, with their ecological notes. Bull. Biogeogr. Soc. Japan 66: 61–73.

OHASHI, Y. and MOTOMURA, H. 2011. Pleuronectiform fishes of northern Kagoshima Prefecture, Japan. Nat. Kagoshima 37: 71–118. (free PDF available at http://www.kagoshima-nature.org/)

SENOU, H., MATSUURA, K. and SHINOHARA, G. 2006. Checklist of fishes in the Sagami Sea with zoogeographical comments on shallow water fishes occurring along the coastlines under the influence of the Kuroshio Current. Mem. Natl. Sci. Mus., Tokyo 41: 389–542.

TASHIRO, S. and MOTOMURA, H. 2015. First record of *Halicampus spinirostris* (Gasterosteiformes: Syngnathidae) from Yaku-shima island in the Osumi Islands, Kagoshima, Japan. Nat. Kagoshima 41: 37–39. (free PDF available at http://www.kagoshima-nature.org/)

YONEZAWA, T., SHINOMIYA, A. and MOTOMURA, H. 2010. Freshwater fishes of Yaku-shima Island, Kagoshima Prefecture, southern Japan. In: MOTOMURA, H. and MATSUURA, K. (eds.), Fishes of Yaku-shima Island – A World Heritage island in the Osumi Group, Kagoshima Prefecture, southern Japan, pp. 249–261. Natl. Mus. Nat. Sci., Tokyo. (free PDF available at http://www.museum.kagoshima-u.ac.jp/staff/motomura/dl_en.html)

YOSHIDA, T. 2013. Pseudochromidae. In: MOTOMURA, H., DEWA, S., FURUTA, K. and MATSUURA, K. (eds.), Fishes of Iou-jima and Take-shima islands, Mishima, Kagoshima, Japan, pp. 99–105. Kagoshima Univ. Mus., Kagoshima and Natl. Mus. Nat. Sci., Tsukuba. (free PDF available at http://www.museum.kagoshima-u.ac.jp/staff/motomura/dl.html)

YOSHIDA, T., AIZAWA, M. and MOTOMURA, H. 2011. Seven new records of cardinalfishes (Perciformes: Apogonidae) from Yaku-shima Island, Kagoshima Prefecture, southern Japan. Nat. Kagoshima 37: 119–125. (free PDF available at http://www.kagoshima-nature.org/)

YOSHIDA, T. and MOTOMURA, H. 2014. Description of an unusual specimen of *Aporops bilinearis* SCHULTZ, 1943 from Yaku-shima island, Kagoshima, southern Japan, and comparison with specimens from the Indo-West Pacific. Nat. Kagoshima 40: 35–41. (free PDF available at http://www.kagoshima-nature.org/)

YOSHIDA, T. and MOTOMURA, H. 2015a. Three apogonid fishes from Yaku-shima island, Kagoshima Prefecture, southern Japan. Nat. Kagoshima 41: 57–60. (free PDF available at http://www.kagoshima-nature.org/)

YOSHIDA, T. and MOTOMURA, H. 2015b. First records of an apogonid fish, *Ostorhinchus fleurieu* (Perciformes: Apogonidae), from Japan. Taxa, Proc. Japan. Soc. Syst. Zool. 39: 17–24.

YOSHIDA, T., NAKAMURA, C. and MOTOMURA, H. 2013. Dottyback fishes (Perciformes: Pseudochromidae) of Kagoshima Prefecture, southern Japan. Nat. Kagoshima 39: 31–45. (free PDF available at http://www.kagoshima-nature.org/)

Chapter 12
Review of the Hydrothermal Crab, *Xenograpsus testudinatus* Ng, Huang & Ho, 2000 (Crustacea: Decapoda: Brachyura: Xenograpsidaae) Inhabiting the Adjacent Waters of the Satsunann Islands, Southern Japan

Hiroshi SUZUKI, Tatsuki IWASAKI, Yu UTSUNOMIYA and Amami IWAMOTO

1. Introduction

Several hydrothermal vents are known to exist in the innermost area of Kagoshima Bay and in the adjacent waters of the Satsunann Islands, southern Kyushu. The tubeworm *Lamellibrachia satsuma* is known to inhabit this area. Another hydrothermal vent animal found at the Satsunann Islands is the crab *Xenograpsus*, which is reported from the vents at Akuseki-jima Island, Tokara Islands (TAKEDA *et al.* 1993). The local people know already for some time that there are shallow water hydrothermal vents, so-called "Tagiri", around Showa-Io-jima Island, about 3 km east of Satsuma-Io-jima Island, Mishima Village, Kagoshima Prefecture. In May 2011, divers and the crew of the Nippon Housou Kyoukai (NHK) were filming at these vents south of Showa-Io-jima Island for a television program. During the process, they found and collected some crab specimens from around the vents and brought them to the laboratory of the first author in Kagoshima University. Subsequently, the crab specimens were identified as *Xenograpsus testudinatus* (NG *et al.* 2014).

The genus *Xenograpsus* was established by TAKEDA and KURATA (1977) as a new genus belonging to the family Grapsidae based on the new species *Xenograpsus novaeinsularis* as a type species. TAKEDA and KURATA (1977) described *X. novaeinsularis* on the basis of two male specimens and one female specimen collected near shallow water volcanic vents at Nishino-shima Island at the Ogasawara Islands. The new volcanic island (named as Nishino-shima-shinto) was first formed in 1973 at the southeastern side of Nishino-shima Island, and in 1974, the old and new islands became united as one single island. The coastline of Nishino-shima Island was scraped off by strong waves, and steep cliffs formed as a result (MURANO 1975, KIDO and KOIKE 1975, NAKAMURA and KOIKE 1975, YAMAZI and WAKAMIYA 1975, TAKEDA and KURATA 1977). In 1993, *X. novaeinsularis* was rediscovered at Akuseki-jima Island, Tokara Islands, in the south of Kyushu, as well as at Kita-Io-jima Island, Io Islands, to the south of the Ogasawara Islands (TAKEDA *et al.* 1993). However, on the basis of the characteristics discussed by NG *et al.* (2000, 2007), the Kyushu specimens, including the Showa-Io-jima Island specimens, agree best with *X. testudinatus* (NG *et al.* 2014). The taxonomic study for higher categories has also been conducted and the new family Xenograpsidae was established based on this genus in 2007 (NG *et al.* 2007). Currently,

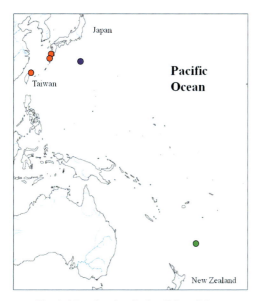

Fig. 1. Map showing the localities of three *Xenograpsus* species found. Red circle: *X. testudinatus*; blue circle: *X. novaeinsularis*; and green circle: *X. ngatama*.

the superfamily Grapsoidea is believed to be composed of seven families.

As mentioned above, taxonomic and systematic studies on *X. testudinatus* were conducted by several researchers. However, the biology, ecology, and distribution of the species have not generally been studied. Although there is little information available, we wish to introduce the interesting and rare crab *X. testudinatus* in this paper, based on existing knowledge including the results obtained from our recent studies conducted at the Satsunann Islands.

2. Geological distribution of *Xenograpsus* species

To date, there are three known species in the genus *Xenograpsus* Takeda & Kurata, 1977: *X. novaeinsularis* TAKEDA and KURATA, 1977, from Kita-Io-jima Island, Ogasawara Islands (= Bonin Islands), Japan, and the Mariana Arc (TAKEDA and KURATA 1977, TÜRKAY and SAKAI 1995); *X. testudinatus* Ng, Huang & Ho, 2000, from Gueishan Island, northern Taiwan (NG et al. 2000), and from Showa-Io-jima Island and Akuseki-jima Island, southern Japan (NG et al. 2014); and *X. ngatama* McLay, 2007, Brothers Seamount, near Kermadec Island, from New Zealand (MCLAY 2007) (Fig. 1). Their localities are on three ridges; that of *X. novaeinsularis* is on the southern edge of Shichito-Io-jima Ridge on the western side of the Ogasawara Basin, those of *X. testudinatus* are on both the north eastern and south western ends of Nansei-shoto Ridge on the southern side of the Okinawa Basin, and that of *X. ngamata* is at the northern edge of Kermadec Ridge, west of the Kermadec Basin. Currently, the three *Xenograpsus* species are found only in the Pacific Ocean. There are, however, many marine ridges, and more hydrothermal vents and associated *Xenograpsus* species are possibly present in the ocean.

It is known, for example, that some hydrothermal vents are located at the mouth of Kagoshima Bay, just off Yamagawa Bay, and at Kuchinoerabu-jima Island and Kodakara-jima Island on Nansei-shoto Ridge. In October 2015, the authors conducted a preliminary survey in Kodakara-jima Island and as a result no *Xenograpsus* crab was found. Future detailed studies on the distribution of *Xenograpsus* species will likely discover new localities at the Satsunann Islands on western edge of the Pacific.

3. Morphology of *Xenograpsus testudinatus*

As mentioned by TAKEDA and KURATA (1977), the general carapace shape of *Xenograpsus* is similar to that of *Planes* crabs. The diagnostic characters of *Xenograpsus* are, however, the same as those of the *Varuna* spp.; namely, they have a ridge running parallel to the infraorbital margin, the broad third maxillipeds that close the buccal cavern entirely, and in males, the narrow abdomen with an elongated terminal segment.

The carapace of *Xenograpsus* is quadratic, almost rounded, and slightly broader than long (Fig. 2 A, B). Its surface is finely granular, punctate with posterolateral striations, and glabrous. Epigastric cristae on the carapace are granulated and distinct. Frontal margin has distinct median cleft. Anterolateral margins are short and oblique, and have single low obscure epibranchial tooth. Posterolateral margins are subparallel. Infraorbital border bears large granules and has deep incision at inner one-third (Fig. 2 C). Suborbital ridge consists of minute granules. Endostomial ridge is prominent and granulated. Posterior margin of epistome is entire and granulated, but lacks lobulation. Third maxilliped is composed of merus and ischium, which are subrectangular and broad, closing without gape; merus is slightly broader than long, anterior reaches as far as epistome and bears a palp positioned in the middle of its anterior edge. Exopod is normal with well-developed flagellum.

Xenograpsus testudinatus has an obscure low tooth on the anterolateral margin, whereas a distinct tooth is present in *X. novaeinsularis* and *X. ngatama* (NG et al. 2007, MCLAY 2007). This is the case even for small specimens of *X. testudinatus*. Although there is a slight angle formed by the juncture of antero- and postero-lateral margins in *X. testudinatus*, this never develops into a low tooth (Fig. 2 and see NG et al, 2007).

Some variations are associated with size in

Fig. 2. *Xenograpsus testudinatus*. A, dorsal view of male; B, dorsal view of female; C, frontal view of male; D, ventral view of male; E, ventral view of female; F, close-up of the tip of chelipeds of male; G, Live crab covered with sulphur-bacteria from Showa Io-jima Island; and H, live crab covered with sulphur-bacteria from Akuseki-jima Island.

X. testudinatus. In larger specimens, the dorsal carapace surface is generally more convex, the frontal margin is more strongly lobulated, and the cardiac and epi-gastric cristae are relatively less distinct.

Ambulatory legs are flattened, short, stout, and unarmed, and they have depressed granulated margins (Fig. 2 A, B). Upper surface of first

3 carpi bear 2 separated longitudinal rows of granulated linear ridges distally, and posterior ridge of carpi bears fringe of silky long setae along anterior ridge. First to third propodi bear 2 granulated ridges along anterior border, and a longitudinal row of silky long setae are present throughout the length of the shallow median depression. Last propodus without median row of setae but densely setose along both borders. Dactyli are broad, short, and sparsely setose, bearing 2 granulated ridges along both borders. Tips of all dactyli curved, heavily pectinate. Male abdomen (Fig. 2 D) is triangular. Telson is triangular and widely elongated with rounded tip. Female abdomen (Fig. 2 E) is large and rounded. Telson is transversely triangular, and its distal margin is medially concave.

Chelipeds are robust, short, equal, similar to each other, and covered with granules (Fig. 2 A, E, F). Carpus of chelipeds is unarmed. Outer surface of palm bears thick granules in addition to longitudinal rows of granules. Its inner surface has a strong protuberance near the proximal end. The inner surface is deeply excavated. Distal part of cutting edge forms pectinate margin with subapical brush of setae on fingertip. The Japanese name "Houki-gani" originated from this brush of setae on fingertip. Some specimens, however, lack this brush (Fig. 2 F).

Live specimens are reddish-brown overall, with the borders of the carapace and legs bright red. Some of them are covered with soft white organisms which may be sulphur-bacteria (Fig. 2 G, H). It is said that the *Xenograpsus* crabs sometimes feed on the bacteria (JENG *et al.* 2004b).

4. Habitat of *Xenograpsus testudinatus*

This species has been found only in relatively shallow hydrothermal vent environments so far

Fig. 3. The photographs showing the seafloor of Showa Io-jima Island (A), Akuseki-jima Island (B), and Kodakara-jima Island (C and D).

(TAKEDA et al. 1993, TÜRKAY and SAKAI 1995). All *Xenograpsus* crabs are reported to be found in areas with submarine volcanoes and/or bubbles coming from volcanic vents (TAKEDA and KURATA 1977, NG et al. 2000, MCLAY 2007). Therefore it is thought that they depend on hydrothermal vents as habitats. *Xenograpsus testudinatus* was found in very high densities in shallow water around sulphur-rich hydrothermal vents. These shallow water vents were discovered in 1997, and they are a part of the Okinawa Trough (KIDO and KOIKE 1975, LEE et al. 1980, KUO 2001, JENG et al. 2004b).

In the area of the Showa Io-jima Island, crabs were found on the bottom surface, in cracks, and behind mounds of volcanic rocks 2 to 3 m in height located at approximately 5 m depth. The mounds are covered by sand and pebbles, with constant streams of bubbles (Fig. 3 A). The total sulphide concentration measured was 0.3 ppm within the bubbles. The hydrothermal vent areas are covered with algae and iron hydroxide and sulphide deposits. In the area of Akuseki-jima Island crabs were found to inhabit similar conditions in about 9 m depth (Fig. 3 B). The pH value of the sea water was measured, and it showed an average of 6.1 with a standard deviation of 0.03 in the area of Showa Io-jima Island. This value is lower than that of ordinary sea water (approximately pH 8.3).

The discharges of this system are sulphur-rich and highly acidic, resulting in a low seawater pH. It was demonstrated that vent discharges with high sulphide levels are integral to the establishment of a chemolithotrophic food-web and/or growth of sulphur-bacteria mats (STÜBEN et al. 1992, DANDO et al. 1995). These food sources are absent in Gueishan Island and Showa Io-jima Island, with shallow water vent discharges having a high concentration of elemental sulphur (99.5% purity) instead (JENG et al. 2004b). Because most of the area is covered with sulphur and the waters contain high concentrations of toxic volcanic gases, it is not surprising that the habitat is species-poor. The only macro-invertebrate associated with these vents is *Xenograpsus testudinatus*. Some fishes, however, were observed in the area of Showa Io-jima Island at times. Some amphipod species were also collected together with *X. testudinatus* in the area. Nevertheless, many fishes, including moray eels, were observed in the area of Kodakara-jima Island, where very few gas bubbles were observed (Fig. 3 C, D).

Lower pH values were found near vents or on the seafloor, whereas those in the water column and far from vents were nearly equal 8.0 pH. The lower pH values resulted from the sulphide in the gas bubbles coming out of the vents, but their effect range might be narrow. The high sulphide levels might not affect the wider area. Future studies are required to determine to which degree the lower pH/high sulphide water affects the distribution of *X. testudinatus*. Moreover, seawater with low pH resulting from volcanic gases may affect the presence or absence of the *Xenograpsus* crabs indirectly. For example, fish and other predators may avoid the low-pH seawater and thereby create more favourable conditions for *Xenograpsus* crabs. These hypotheses require future studies.

Furthermore, the temperature of the water column above vents is a few degrees higher than that of the surrounding seawater. The conditions on the seafloor are even more severe, with around 40 degrees Centigrade at 1 cm depth inside the substrate. The higher temperatures in the substrate may support the high density, rapid maturation, and rapid growth of *Xenograpsus*. This topic also requires additional research.

5. Food of *Xenograpsus testudinatus*

The crabs swarm out of their crevices during slack tide to feed on dead zooplankton (or marine snow) resulting from the toxic plumes discharged by the vents. Such feeding behaviour was the first ever reported for any hydrothermal vent species (JENG et al. 2004b). Similar feeding behaviour was observed in the Japanese population of *X. testudinatus* under natural conditions. However, the crabs feed also on frozen mysids and artificial food under aquarium conditions. *Xenograpsus testudinatus* may be carnivorous and a scavenger like other grapsoid crabs.

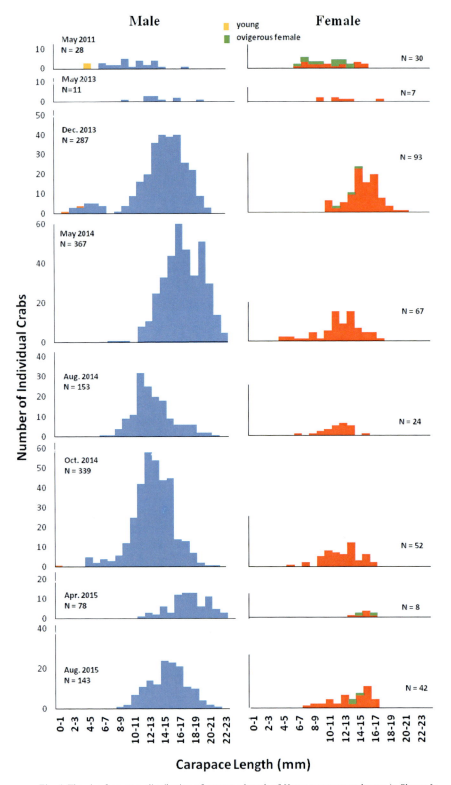

Fig. 4. The size frequency distribution of carapace length of *Xenograpsus testudinatus* in Showa Iojima Island.

6. Reproduction and amount of individuals of *X. testudinatus*

Although only few aspects of the biology of *X. testudinatus* were investigated, its feeding ecology was reported by JENG et al. (2004b) and the larval development was studied by JENG et al. (2004a). The other biological and ecological characteristics of *X. testudinatus* have not been investigated to date. A study on the population ecology of *X. testudinatus* was conducted in the restricted area near Showa Io-jima Island. The study offers some information about the total number of individuals in the habitat and their reproduction.

The crab distribution is concentrated in a small area of approximately 100 m × 50 m, located on the southern coast of Showa Io-jima Island. The total number of individuals of *X. testudinatus* was estimated to be approximately 3500 (3258–3717), using a marking-recapture method (Table 1). This estimated number of crabs may be enough to keep the population. The reveal of recruitment mechanism may be one of research themes for *Xenograpsus* crabs being distributed in sporadically.

The size of *X. testudinatus* males ranged from 3.45 to 22.40 mm in carapace length (CL) and that of females ranged from 5.25 to 18.40 mm in CL (Fig. 4). The smallest ovigerous female was 6.0 mm in carapace length, suggesting high fecundity and early larval production (TÜRKAY and SAKAI 1995). Unfortunately, an accurate reproductive season has never been revealed, but it is thought to be April to August. Further studies focussing on this topic should be carried out.

Acknowledgements

We are especially grateful to captain A. HABANO and the crew of the Training Vessel "Nansei-Maru", Miss. M. MATSUOKA, technical staff of the Faculty of Fisheries, and Mr. K. KAJIWARA, fisherman in Satsuma Io-jima, for their kind assistance in collecting crab specimens. This study was supported in part by Grants-in-Aid for the Core Program from the president of Kagoshima University.

References

DANDO, P. R., HUGHES, J. A. and THIERMANN, F. 1995. Preliminary observations on biological communities at shallow hydrothermal vents in the Aegean Sea. In: Parson, L. M., WALKER, D. R. and DIXON, C. L. (eds.), Hydrothermal vents and processes. Geological Society Special Publication No. 87, pp. 303–317. Geological Society, London.

JENG, M.-S., CLARK, P. F. and NG. P. K. L. 2004a. The first zoea, megalopa, and first crab stage of the hydrothermal vent crab, *Xenograpsus testudinatus* (Decapoda: Brachyura: Grapsoidea) and systematic implications for the Varunidae. Journal of Crustacean Biology 24: 188–212.

JENG, M.-S., NG, N. K. and NG. P. K. L. 2004b. Hydrothermal vent crabs feeds on marine snow. Nature 432: 969.

KIDO, T., and KOIKE, Y. 1975. On the survey in the inlet of "Nisinosima-Sin To". Journal of Tokyo University, Fisheries 61(1–2): 41–47, figs. 1–5. (in Japanese with English abstract).

KUO, F. W. 2001. Preliminary investigations of the hydrothermal activities off Kueishan Island. M.Sc. thesis, Institute of Marine Geology and Chemistry, National Sun Yat Sen University, Kaohsiung. (in Chinese with English abstract, unpublished).

LEE, C. S., SHOR, G. G., BIBEE Jr., L. D. Lu, R. S. and HILDE, Y. W. C. 1980. Okinawa Trough: Origin of a back-arc basin. Marine Geology 35: 219–241.

McLAY C. L. 2007. New crabs from hydrothermal vents of the Kermadec Ridge submarine volcanoes, New Zealand: *Gandalfus* gen. nov. (Bythograeidae) and *Xenograpsus* (Varunidae) (Decapoda: Brachyura). Zootaxa 1524: 1–22.

MURANO M. 1975. Phytoplankton in the waters surrounding a new active volcanic island, Nisinosima-Sin-To. Journal of Tokyo University, Fisheries 61(1–2): 93–107. (in Japanese with English abstract).

NAKAMURA, Y. and KOIKE, Y. 1975. On the change of the bottom topography in the surrounding area of the island Nisino-sima. Journal of Tokyo University, Fisheries 61(1–2): 37–40, fig. 1–3. (in Japanese with English abstract).

NG, N. K., HUANG, J.F. and HO, P.H. 2000. Description of a new species of hydrothermal crab, *Xenograpsus testudinatus* (Crustacea: Decapoda: Brachyura: Grapsidae). In: Hwang, J.-S., Wang, C.-H., Chan, T.-Y. (eds.), Proceedings of the International Symposium on Marine Biology in Taiwan, pp. 191–199, figs 1–3.

Table 1. The results of two trials using the marking-recapture method.

	Total number of individuals			
	marked and released	captured	recaptured	estimated
First trial	328	34	3	3717
Second trial	357	146	16	3257

Crustacean and Plankton Taxonomy, Ecology and Living Resources. 26–27 May, 1998, Taiwan. National Taiwan Museum Special Series, No. 10, National Taiwan Museum, Taipei.

NG, N. K., DAVIE, P. J. F., SCHUBART, C. D. and NG, P. K. L. 2007. Xenograpsidae, a new family of grapsoid crabs (Crustacea: Brachyura) associated with shallow water hydrothermal vents. Raffles Bulletin of Zoology, Supplement Number 16: 233–256.

NG, N. K., SUZUKI, H., SHIH, H.-T., DEWA, S.-I., and NG P. K. L. 2014. The hydrothermal crab, *Xenograpsus testudinatus* NG, HUANG & HO, 2000 (Crustacea: Decapoda: Brachyura: Grapsidae) in southern Japan. Proceedings of the Biological Society of Washington, 127 (2): 391–399.

STÜBEN, D., BLOOMER, S. H., Taïbi, N. E., NEUMANN, BENDEL, T. H., V., PUSCHEL, U., BARONE, A., LANGE, A., Li, S. WU, C., and ZHANG, D. 1992. First results of study of sulphur rich hydrothermal activity from an island-arc environment: Esmeralda Bank in the Mariana Arc. Marine Geology 103: 521–528.

TAKEDA, M., and KURATA, Y. 1977. Crabs of the Ogasawara Islands. IV. A collection made at the new volcanic island, Nishino-shima-shinto, in 1975. Bulletin of National Science Museum (A) Zoology 3(2): 91–111, figs. 1–9.

TAKEDA, M., TAKEUCHI, H. and SUGANUMA, H. 1993. Occurrence of *Xenograpsus novaeinsularis* Takeda & Kurata (Crustacea: Decapoda: Brachyura) in the Tokara and Iwo Islands. Nature and Environmental Science Research 6: 59–64. (in Japanese with English abstract).

TÜRKAY, M., and SAKAI, K. 1995. Decapods crustaceans from a volcanic hot spring in the Marianas. Senckenbergiana maritima 26 (1/2): 5–35.

YAMAZI, I., and WAKAMIYA, M. 1975. Zooplankton in the waters surrounding a new active volcanic island, Nisinosima-Sin-To. Journal of Tokyo University Fisheries 61(1–2): 71–92. (in Japanese with English abstract).

Chapter 13
Study on the Marine Natural Products Chemistry of the Red Alga, *Hanayanagi*, in the Osumi Islands

Toshiyuki HAMADA, Satoaki ONITSUKA and Hiroaki OKAMURA

1. Introduction

Organisms have undergone a tremendous amount of evolution since they first came into existence approximately 3,500 million years ago. Through an evolutionary process beginning with unicellular organism, which later developed into multicellular organisms, they have acquired more complex cellular processes, and have adapted to their environment. This adaptation includes the biosynthesis of primary and secondary metabolites. Metabolites directly involved in normal growth, development, and reproduction are referred to as primary metabolites, and include amino acids, proteins, sugars, and nucleic acids. However, secondary metabolites are organic compounds that might not be absolutely required for survival, since their absence does not result in immediate death, although a lack of these metabolites could cause long-term impairment of the organism's fitness.

Secondary metabolites often play an important role in protection, competition, and other interactions between species. In terms of protection, these metabolites serve as a mechanism to provide chemical defense for the organism against predators, bacteria, fungi, and viruses. In addition, secondary metabolites could affect the behavior or physiology among individuals of the same species, in which case these chemicals are referred to as pheromones and chemical signals. From a medical perspective, many researchers are particularly interested in secondary metabolites due to their wide spectrum of potential biological activities. Extensive effort has been focused on bioprospecting bioactive molecules from natural resources and this research field is referred to as Natural Products Chemistry.

In order to discover new medicines, including novel drugs for cancer treatment, and to clarify the role of secondary metabolites in ecosystems, our research group has focused on secondary metabolites from the medical herbs and marine invertebrates of southern Japan. As a part of this ongoing research, we have studied the secondary metabolites produced by the red alga commonly referred to as "*hanayanagi*". Here, we introduce *hanayanagi* and its secondary metabolites, followed by our main aim and the current progress completed in this research project.

2. The red alga *hanayanagi*

The marine red alga commonly known as *hanayanagi* has the scientific name *Chondria armata* (Kützing) Okamura, and belongs to the family Rhodomelaceae. In this species, many individuals (ranging in height from 5 to 6 cm) extend straight from a thick husk-shaped appressorium. The lower parts of this alga are pillar shaped, 2–3 mm in diameter, and their upper portion is irregularly divided into several thin branches. They grow and spread over rocks in the lower intertidal zone (Red Data Book of Kagoshima Prefecture 2016). According to AlgaeBase (http://www.algaebase.org/), *hanayanagi* is found in tropical and sub-tropical regions, in particular in East Asia (Japan, China, and Taiwan), Southeast Asia (Indonesia, Myanmar, the Philippines, and Vietnam), Southwest Asia (India, the Laccadive Islands, and Sri Lanka), Africa (Kenya, Mauritius, Mozambique, South Africa, and Tanzania), as well as Oceania (Australia, Central Polynesia, Fiji, Papua New Guinea, and the Solomon Islands). In Japan, this alga is distributed from the Pacific coast in southern Honshu to the Nansei Islands including the coastal area of Kagoshima. The Kagoshima region includes three climatic zones (tropical, sub-tropical, and warm-temperature) (NISHIMURA 1981). Previous surveys have confirmed the distribution of *hanayanagi* around Tokuno-shima and Okinoerabu-jima Islands in the tropical zone, Tanega-shima, Yaku-shima, and Koshiki-jima Islands in the sub-tropical zone, and Naga-shima Island and Ushinohama beach (Akune City) in the warm-temperature zone. Additionally, *hanayanagi* has been used as a vermifuge in the Amami and Ryukyu Islands. Its fly-killing properties were previously known to the inhabitants of Yaku-shima Island, Kagoshima.

3. *Hanayanagi* Metabolites

The study of secondary metabolites from *hanayanagi* began with the discovery of an anthelmintic domoic acid (**1**) in the 1960s by DAIGO, along with D-aspartic acid and L-citrulline (DAIGO 1959); however, only a few studies on compounds from this organism have been published. The following review of previous studies summarizes the metabolites that have been reported from *hanayanagi*.

Domoic acid, referred to as "doumoi", a local name for *hanayanagi* in Tokuno-shima, is a biotoxic amino acid. Its chemical structure was confirmed to be (2*S*,3*S*,4*S*)-2-carboxy-4-[(1*Z*,3*E*,5*R*)-5-carboxy-1-methyl-1,3-hexadienyl] pyrrolidine-3-acetic acid (Fig. 1; DAIGO 1959). This compound showed extremely strong insecticidal activity, similar to that of α-kainic acid (**2**) isolated from another Rhodomelaceae alga *Digenea simplex*. In Canada during 1987, an extensive amnesic shellfish poisoning (ASP) event occurred due to the ingestion of a cultured mussel. The causative agent was determined to be domoic acid, which was produced by the diatom *Pseudonitzschia pungens* f. *multiseries* (BATES 1989). Although it was thought that *P. pungens* produced domoic acid, ARAKAWA's group proved the red alga *C. armata* (*hanayanagi*) itself has the ability to produce domoic acid when cultured in the laboratory (JIANG 2014).

Following the discovery of domoic acid (**1**), Japanese researchers reported the isolation of domoic acid-related metabolites from the 1990s through the 2000s (Fig. 1). The isodomoic acids A (**3**), B (**4**), and C (**5**), as well as the domoilactones A (**6**) and B (**7**) were isolated from *C. armata* collected off the coast of Yaku-shima Island,

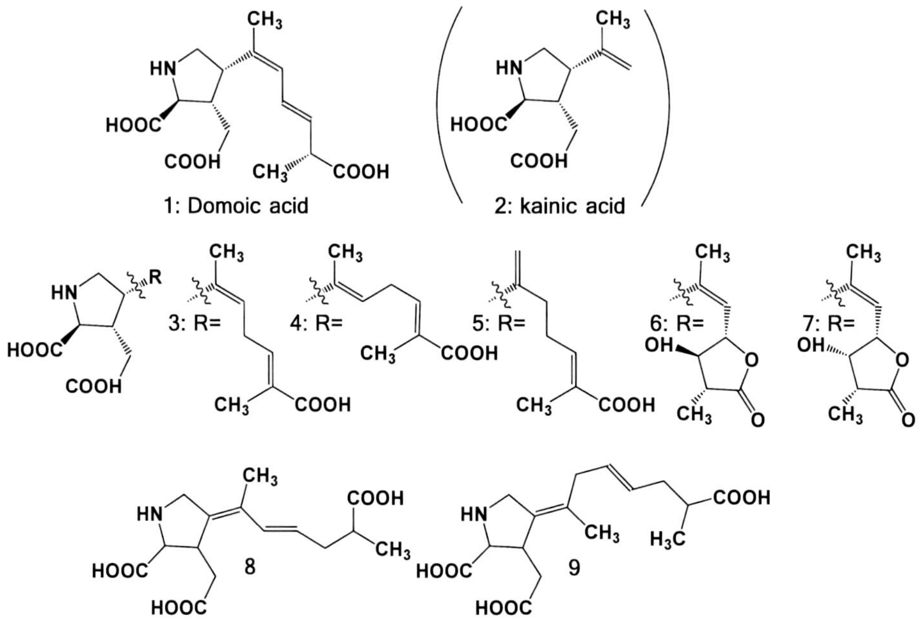

Fig. 1. Domoic acid derivatives isolated from Japanese *hanayanagi*.

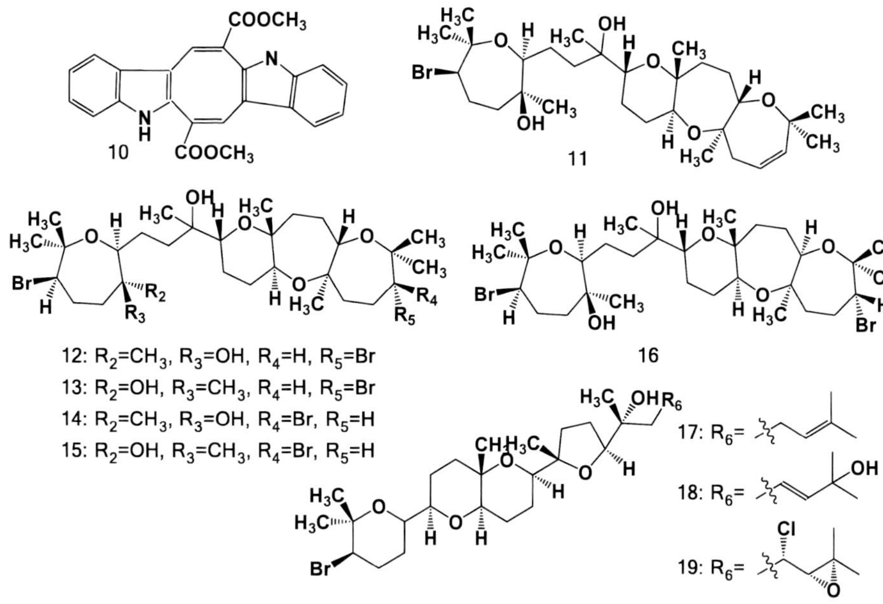

Fig. 2. Metabolites isolated from Indian and Australian *hanayanagi*.

Kagoshima in the 1990s (MAEDA 1986, 1987). These metabolites showed strong insecticidal activity against the American cockroach. Furthermore, the isodomoic acids G (**8**) and H (**9**) were isolated from the same alga collected at Hanasezaki, Kagoshima by ARAKAWA's group (ZAMAN 1997). The structures of these metabolites were deduced based on nuclear magnetic resonance (NMR) spectral analyses.

Since 1999, Indian researchers have isolated metabolites other than domoic acid derivatives (Fig. 2) from *C. armata*. GOVENKAR and WAHIDULLA have studied the fatty acid composition in *C. armata* collected from Anjuna, Goa, India. (GOVENKAR 1999). Using gas chromatography-mass spectrometry (GC-MS), saturated fatty acids (such as n-tetradecanoic acid, *n*-pentadecanoic acid, *n*-hexadecanoic acid and *n*-octadecanoic acid), and unsaturated fatty acids (such as hexadec-5-enoic acid, hexadec-4-enoic acid and octadec-9-enoic acid) were identified from the petroleum ether soluble fraction of this alga. The same research group also identified free sterols such as cholest-5-en-3β-ol, 24-methylene cholest-5-en-3β-ol, 23ε-methyl cholest-5-en-3β-ol, 23ε-methyl 5α-cholestan-3β-ol, 24β-ethyl cholest-5,22-diene-3β-ol, and 24β-ethyl cholest-5-ene-3β-ol (GOVENKAR and WAHIDULLA 2000a), and the fatty ester, pentyl hentriacontanoate, as well as the orange red pigment, caulerpin (**10**), from the same source (GOVENKAR and WAHIDULLA 2000b). In 2001, CIAVATTA's group isolated six new bromotriterpene polyethers, the armatols A-F (**11-16**), from the Indian Ocean (off the coast of Anjuna) from *C. armata* (CIAVATTA 2001). Additionally, the total synthesis of armatol F was carried out previously (FUJIWARA 2010). In addition, glycolipids have also been identified by WAHIDULLA group (AL-FADHLI 2006). The structures of (2R)-2-O-(5,8,11,14-eicosatetranoyl)-3-O-α-D-galactopyranosyl-*sn*-glycerol and its pentacetate, as well as (2R)-1-O-(palmitoyl)-2-O-(5,8,11,14,17-eicosapentanoyl)-3-O-β-D-galactopyranosyl-*sn*-glycerol (GL$_3$) were elucidated by multi-dimensional NMR and electrospray ionization mass spectrometry (ESI-MS). Recently, Australian researchers isolated three new brominated triterpene polyethers, aplysiols C-E (**17-19**) from the Orpheus Island, Queensland, Australia (OLA 2010; Fig. 2). Their structures were determined by comparison with the related metabolite, aplysiol B, which was previously reported from the anaspidean mollusk Aplysia dactylomela. Six known metabolites, including two brominated diterpenes, (-)-*ent*-angasiol and its acetate, as well as three brominated C15 acetogenin acetylenic ethers ((-)-pinnatifidenyne, (+)-laurenyne, (+)-obtusenyne), and the symmetrical halogenated triterpene polyether, intricatetraol, were also isolated from the same species.

Surprisingly, palytoxin (PTX; **20**, Fig. 3) was also isolated from *hanayanagi* (MORI 2016). The PTX in this alga was identified using NMR and MS. In 1971, PTX was first isolated from a zoanthid, *Palythoa toxica* (MOORE 1971), and the congeners were isolated from several marine organisms, such as zoanthids, fish, crabs, cyanobacteria, and dinoflagellates (FUKUI 1987; YASUMOTO 1986; NAKAJIMA 1981; KERBRAT 2011; USAMI 1995); however, the original producer has not been determined. Identification of the original producer of PTX is essential to further investigate its bioconcentration in marine ecosystems, and to stop this molecule from ultimately leading to food poisoning.

4. Aim of the *hanayanagi* studies in the area around the Osumi Islands

We are currently undertaking the isolation and structure determination of secondary metabolites isolated from *hanayanagi* collected off the coast of Hanasezaki (Minami-kyushu City) and Harutahama (Yaku-shima Island), Kagoshima, Japan. The same alga from different places in the Kagoshima area will be collected in the near future. The purpose of this project is to search for new domoic acid derivatives and palytoxin derivatives, and to clarify the mechanisms that cause ecosystemic changes among marine organisms in the Islands of Kagoshima, especially changes in the intra- and inter-climatic regions, which can be accomplished using the data concerning secondary metabolite production.

The dinoflagellate genus *Ostreopsis* is a potential producer of palytoxin derivatives,

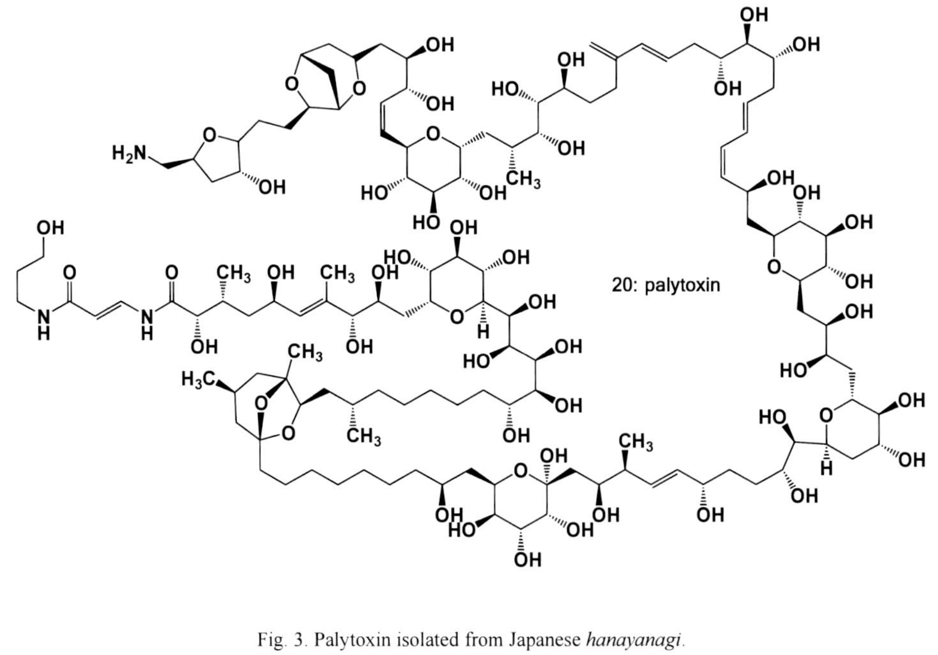

Fig. 3. Palytoxin isolated from Japanese *hanayanagi*.

including the ovatoxins. Phylogenetic analyses determined that the Japanese *Ostreopsis* should be divided into 4 types: the strongly toxic type A, highly toxic types B and C, and non-toxic type D (Sato 2011). In the areas around Kyushu and Shikoku, types A and B are found, while the non-toxic type D is only distributed in the Okinawa region. These data indicate that the structure and toxicity of palytoxin derivatives must be different between the southern and northern areas of Japan. It is noteworthy that ciguatera fish poisoning related to the dinoflagellate genus *Gambierdiscus*, is present as two types (type 1 and type 2) and is distributed along coastal areas in Japan (Kuno 2010). Type 1 is distributed in tropical and subtropical areas (Okinawa and Amami Islands), while the non-toxic type 2 is distributed in warm-temperate areas (Shikoku and Honshu areas). This distribution might be related to different types of ciguatoxins (CTXs). While CTX3C is found in the Miyazaki prefecture, CTX1B is located in the Okinawa prefecture and Amami area. Similar to the CTXs, there is a distinct distribution between the relevant southern and northern symbionts. The dinoflagellate genus *Ostreopsis* (a candidate producer of palytoxin) and the diatom *P. pungens* (a candidate producer of domoic acid) can be distinguished by chemical structure analysis of their respective metabolites. Motomura (2015) proposed that a new biogeographical boundary line for marine fishes located between Yaku-shima Island and a group of Io-jima, Take-shima, and Tanega-shima Islands (refer to the Motomura's review in this book). The metabolomic analysis of *hanayanagi* in the Osumi Islands and the Kagoshima mainland is required to assess the location of the biogeographical boundary line of marine organisms in the Osumi Islands, in addition to the fishes.

5. Conclusion

There are currently few reports concerning the secondary metabolites isolated from *hanayanagi*. Japanese researchers have reported the isolation of domoic acid derivatives (**1**, **3-9**) and palytoxin (**20**), while Indian researchers have undertaken the isolation of metabolites including polyethers (**11-16**), and Australian researchers isolated brominated triterpene polyethers (**17-19**). The isolation and the structure elucidation of secondary metabolites from *hanayanagi* collected off the Kagoshima coast are currently in progress.

Acknowledgments

We are grateful to Dr. T. Yasumoto (Japan Food Research Laboratories), Dr. N. Fusetani (Fisheries and Oceans Hakodate), Dr. O. Arakawa (Nagasaki University), and Dr. R. Terada (Kagoshima University) for helpful comments and encouragement. We thank K. Kobayashi, Y. Motoi, A. Kariyazaki, K. Yamashita, K. Imaizumi, M. Ide, R. Sugita and T. Oomuraya (Graduate School of Science and Engineering, Kagoshima University) for technical support, as well as H. Kitahara for writing assistance.

We are thankful to the Research Center for the Pacific Islands at Kagoshima University for providing the opportunity to survey Yaku-shima Island. This work was supported by the Cooperative Research Program of the "Network Joint Research Centre for Materials and Devices" (No. 2011287 and 2014440), and the "Establishment of Research and Education Network on Biodiversity and Its Conservation in the Satsunan Islands" project of Kagoshima University adopted by the Ministry of Education, Culture, Sports, Science and Technology, Japan.

References

Al-Fadhli, A., Wahidulla, S. and D'souza, L. 2006. Glycolipids from the red alga *Chondria armata* (Kutz.) Okamura. Glycobiology 16: 902–915.

Bates, S., Bird, C., Defreitas, A., Foxall, R., Gilgan, M., Hanic, L., Johnson, G., Mcculloch, A., Odense, P. and Pocklington, R. 1989. Pennate diatom nitzschia-pungens as the primary source of domoic acid, a toxin in shellfish from eastern prince edward island, Canada. Canadian Journal of Fisheries and Aquatic Science 46: 1203–1215.

Böttinger, H., Beress, L. and Habermann, E. 1986. Involvement of $(Na^+ + K^+)$-ATPase in binding and actions of palytoxin on human-erythrocytes. Biochim. Biophys. Acta 861: 164–176.

Ciavatta, M. L., Wahidulla, S., D'souza, L., Scognamiglio, G. and Cimino, G. 2001. New bromotriterpene polyethers from the Indian alga *Chondria armata*. Tetrahedron 57: 617–623.

Daigo, K. 1959. Studies on the constituents of *Chondria*

armata. II. Isolation of an anthelmintical constituent. and III. Constitution of Domoic Acid. J. Pham. Soc. Japan 79: 350–386.

FUJIWARA, K., HIROSE, Y., SATO, D., KAWAI, H. and SUZUKI, T. 2010. Studies toward the total synthesis of armatol F: stereoselective construction of the C6 and C7 stereocenters and formation of the A-ring skeleton. Tetrahedron Letters 51: 4263–4266.

FUKUI, M., MURATA, M., INOUE, A., GAWEL, M. and YASUMOTO, T. 1987. Occurrence of Palytoxin in the trigger fish *Melichtys-vidua*. Toxicon 25: 1121–1124.

GOVENKAR, M. B. and WAHIDULLA, S. 1999. Studies on the fatty acids of the red alga *Chondria armata* (Kütz.) Okamura. Botanica Marina 42: 3–5.

GOVENKAR, M. B. and WAHIDULLA, S. 2000a. Free sterols of the red alga *Chondria armata* (Kütz.) Okamura. Botanica Marina 43: 201–204.

GOVENKAR, M. B. and WAHIDULLA, S. 2000b. Constituents of *Chondria armata*. Phytochemistry 54: 979–981.

HABERMANN, E. 1989. Palytoxin acts through Na^+,K^+-ATPase. Toxicon 27: 1171–1187.

JIANG, S., KUWANO, K., ISHIKAWA, N., YANO, M., TAKATANI, T. and ARAKAWA, O. 2014. Production of domoic acid by laboratory culture of the red alga *Chondria armata*. Toxicon 92: 1–5.

KERBRAT, A. S., AMZIL, Z., PAWLOWIEZ, R., GOLUBIC, S., SIBAT, M., DARIUS, H. T., CHINAIN, M. and LAURENT, D. 2011. First evidence of palytoxin and 42-hydroxy-palytoxin in the marine cyanobacterium *Trichodesmium*. Mar. Drugs 9: 543–560.

KUNO, S., KAMIKAWA, R., YOSHIMATSU, S., SAGARA, T., NISHIO, S. and SAKO, Y. 2010. Genetic diversity of *Gambierdiscus* spp. (Gonyaulacales, Dinophyceae) in Japanese coastal areas. Phycological Research 58: 44–52.

MAEDA, M., KODAMA, T., TANAKA, T., YOSHIZUMI, H., TAKEMOTO, T., NOMOTO, K. and FUJITA, T. 1986. Structures of isodomoic acids A, B and C, novel insecticidal amino acids from the red alga *Chondria armata*. Pharmaceutical Society of Japan 34: 4892–4895.

MAEDA, M., KODAMA, T., TANAKA, T., YOSHIZUMI, H., TAKEMOTO, T., NOMOTO, K. and FUJITA, T. 1987. Structures of domoilactone A and B, novel amino acids from the red alga *Chondria armata*. Tetrahedron Letter 28: 633–636.

MOORE, R. E. and SCHEUER, P. J. 1971. Palytoxin: a new marine toxin from a coelenterate. Science 172: 495–498.

MORI, S., SUGAHARA, K., MAEDA, M., NOMOTO, K., IWASHITA, T. and YAMAGAKI, T. 2016. Insecticidal activity guided isolation of palytoxin from a red alga, *Chondria armata*. Tetrahedron Letters 57: 3612–3617.

MOTOMURA, H. 2015. Fish species diversity in the Ryukyu Islands. In: Ecol. Soc. Japan (ed.), Biodiversity, formation history, and conservation in the Nansei Islands. Ecology lectures 8, pp. 56–63. Nanpou Shinsya, Kagoshima.

NAKAJIMA, I., OSHIMA, Y. and YASUMOTO, T. 1981. Toxicity of benthic dinoflagellates found in coral-reef. 2. Toxicity of benthic dinoflagellates in Okinawa. Bull. Jpn. Soc. Sci. Fish. 47: 1029–1033.

NISHIMURA, S. 1981. The sea and life on the earth. 284 pp., Kaimeisha, Tokyo.

OLA, A. R. B., BABEY, A. M., MOTTI, C. and BOWDEN, B. F. 2010. Aplysiols C-E, brominated triterpene polyethers from the marine alga *Chondria armata* and a revision of the structure of Aplysiol B. Australian Journal of Chemistry 63: 907–914.

SATO, S., NISHIMURA, T., UEHARA, K., SAKANARI, H., TAWONG, W., HARIGANEYA, N., SMITH, K., RHODES, L., YASUMOTO, T. and TAIRA, Y. 2011. Phylogeography of *Ostreopsis* along west Pacific coast, with special reference to a novel clade from Japan. PLoS ONE 6: e27983.

USAMI, M., SATAKE, M., ISHIDA, S., INOUE, A., KAN, Y. and YASUMOTO, T. 1995. Palytoxin analogs from the dinoflagellate *Ostreopsis siamensis*. J. Am. Chem. Soc. 117: 5389–5390.

YASUMOTO, T., YASUMURA, D., OHIZUMI, Y., TAKAHASHI, M., ALCALA, A. C. and ALCALA, L. C. 1986. Palytoxin in 2 species of xanthid crab from the Philippines. Agric. Biol. Chem. 50: 163–167.

ZAMAN, L., ARAKAWA, O., SHIMOSU, A., ONOUE, Y., NISHIO, S., SHIDA, Y. and NOGUCHI, T. 1997. Two new isomers of domoic acid from a red alga, *Chondria armata*. Toxicon 35: 205–212.

Chapter 14
Geological Overview of the Shimanto Belt in Tanega-shima Island

Yujin KITAMURA, Naoya SAKAMOTO and Kuniyo KAWABATA

1. Introduction

The Tanega-shima island, a member of the Osumi islands together with the Yaku-shima island and the Mage-shima island, locates in the northern part of the Nansei islands which consists the Ryukyu arc. The Osumi islands are classified as the North Ryukyus that consists of the islands north of the Tokara strait (Kizaki, 1978). The North Ryukyus is characterized by active volcanoes of the Tokara islands that comprises the volcanic front from Mt. Kirishima via Mt. Sakurajima, Mt. Kaimon, Io-jima island to Suwanose island. The Osumi islands locate east of this volcanic chain and are non-volcanic formed by uplift of the basement. The Yaku-shima island was developed in Neogene associated with the uplift of huge granite intrusion occupying central part of the island. Several coastal terraces of sedimentary rocks fringe the granite body other than the northwest coast. These sedimentary rocks turn into hornfels at the contact with the granite. The Tanega-shima island is composed of the basement that is the Paleogene Kumage Group of the southern Shimanto belt, overlain by Miocene Kukinaga group, Pliocene Masuda formation and Quaternary formations.

The Shimanto belt constituting major part of the Osumi islands is an accretionary complex formed in the period from Cretaceous to Neogene and lies along the Pacific coast in the southwest Japan. The accretionary complex is a geological body that formed during the subduction of the oceanic plate beneath the continental plate by accretion that off-scraping and/or underplating the sediments on the surface of the oceanic plate to the overriding plate. In the southwest Japan, accretionary complex is younging toward Pacific coast side and constitute the hanging wall of the plate boundary generating megaearthquakes. Presently evolving accretionary complex lies on the seafloor along the Nankai trough, which is recently being investigated thoroughly in the field of earthquake science by means of, for example, scientific ocean drilling. The Shimanto belt crops out so widely on land that it must be a clue for understanding modern plate boundary processes.

Here we overview the geology of the Osumi islands, especially on the Tanega-shima island, and with some our recent results, present an outlook for the studies on the geochemical quantification of the rock deformation and associated material transfer in the subduction zone.

2. Accretionary Prism

The "accretion" is classified into "off-scraping" that the sediments on the oceanic plate is scraped off by the overrinding plate at relatively shallow depth and "underplating" that they are accreted to the hanging wall plate from below in relatively deeper part. During the both type of accretion, strata are cut by the faults to accrete. In case of the off-scraping, the sediments are yet unconsolidated and thus the faulting is not capable of generating large earthquake, while the underplating is thought to be associated with the bending of the plate boundary fault that may be closely linked with the plate boundary megaearthquake (KITAMURA et al. 2005, KITAMURA and KIMURA 2012). The underplate rocks are highly deformed and present a kind of fault rock called "tectonic mélange". In the Shimanto belt, the geologic bodies of off-scraping and underplating occur alternately.

The investigation of the tectonic mélange in the Shimanto belt in Shikoku, the tectonic mélange represent the deformed fault zone of the plate boundary (KITAMURA et al. 2005). An intensely deformed fault occurs at the top of the tectonic mélange that includes pseudotachylyte which is the glassy material due to frictional melting of the rock during earthquake rupture. This finding results in this fault to be seismogenic, i.e. the source fault of the plate boundary megaearthquake, in the past.

The tectonic mélange which itself is the huge plate boundary fault can be attributed to the slow earthquakes recently revealed by the highly sensitive observations (KITAMURA and KIMURA 2012). As above-mentioned, the rocks from the Shimanto belt is regarded as the excellent record of the plate boundary that arouse megaearthquakes or tiny earthquakes. Thus the geological investigation in the Osumi islands would provide some insights into the seismogenesis and the accretionary complex formation in the region of the Ryukyu trench.

3. Geology in Tanega-shima island
3.1. The Shimanto belt

The geology of the Tanega-shima island is well reviewed by SAKAI (2010). The basement rocks of the Shimanto belt in the Osumi islands have been called as the Kumage group (HANZAWA 1934). The age of the Kumage group is in the range of Middle Eocene to Oligocene (HAYASAKA et al. 1980, 1983, HAYASAKA 1985, OKADA et al. 1982, SAITO et al. 2007, KIKUKAWA et al. 2014). The Kumage group resembles not to the Middle Ryukyus but to the Hyuga and Nichinan group in the south Kyushu with the following characteristics in terms of lithostratography and biostratigraphy: structural arrangement that accretionary complex strata in the northwest and olistostrome strata in the southeast; and the presence of Middle Miocene acidic volcanic rock intrusions and Miocene shallow deposits covering the Shimanto belt strata.

The Kumage group distributes in the Northern Tanega-shima (Kita-Tane) and the west coast of the Southern Tanega-shima (Minami-Tane), and overlain by Pliocene Masuda formation in the Middle Tanega-shima (Naka-Tane) and by Middle Miocene Kukinaga formation in the east of Minami-Tane. HAYASAKA et al. (1983) subdivided the Kumage group based on the geological classification by OKADA et al. (1982) into the Nishinoomote formation, Kadokurasaki formation and Tateishi formation. SAKAI (1992, 2010) set up another classification based on lithofacies and deformation into the Kumage complex and the Kadokurasaki complex, bounded by the inferred fault trending NNE-SSW passing through Hamatsubaki, Naka-Tane. The Kumage complex is a group of strata associated with subduction-accretion that deposit/deformed body with accretion related deformation overlain by weakly deformed/metamorphosed coherent turbidites, where the Kadokurasaki complex is an olistostrome composed of large scale mixed strata of argillaceous rocks lack of clear bedding including various size of blocks randomly. These complexes are compared to the Hyuga group and Nichinan group of the Shimanto belt in the south Kyushu, respectively.

The ages of the Kumage complex and the Kadokurasaki complex were implied by radiolarian fossils Middle to Late Eocene and Middle Eocene, respectively (SUZUKI et al. 1979, OKADA et al. 1982, KUWAZURU and NAGATSU 2007, SAITO et al. 2007). Recent nannofossil study reported Middle Oligocene from the Nishinoomote formation in Kumage complex (KIKUKAWA et al 2014).

The Tateishi formation of the Kumage complex presents the character of accretionary material that shows argillaceous rocks with sheared folds and slaty cleavages. The overlying Nishinoomote formation is weakly metamorphosed coherent turbidites with occurrences of various sedimentary structures and deformations such as sand volcanoes or megaripples (OKADA and WHITAKER 1979), where its depositional condition inferred to be deep marine facies based on the trace fossils (HAYASAKA et al. 1980, FUKUDA and SAKAI 1993). The strata of the Kadokurasaki complex frequently overturns and occurs conglomerate-bearing mudstones, slumping, disturbed bedding, discontinuity of lithofacies, and fossils of shallow marine mollusk (HAYAKAWA et al. 1980, OKADA et al. 1982). SAKAI (1980) examined the occurrence of greenstones in the west coast of Minami-Tane and the east coast of Yaku-shima island, and concluded that these are of the olistostrome.

3.2. Neogene formations

The Kumage group, Shimanto belt is unconformably overlain by Kukinaga group, Masuda formation, Hase formation and Takenokawa formation. The Kukinaga group consists of Tashiro formation, Kawachi formation and Osaki formation, where their depositional age is Early Miocene. These strata distribute in the southeast of the island, are thinning toward north. The Masuda formation, Hase formation and Takenokawa formation unconformably are Quaternary deposits that cover the Tashiro formation and Kawachi formation.

4. Pressure solution deformation in the Shimanto belt

Pressure solution is a phenomenon that when a rock suffered under stress, an excess stress concentrates at the contact between constituting minerals, which consequences dissolution, diffusion and precipitation at a distance. It is often observable as a black seam, the pressure solution seam, in the rock thin section under optical microscope.

The isocon method is a procedure of estimating rock deformation through volume change based on the chemical composition data, proposed by GREESENS (1967) and established by GRANT (1986). KAWABATA et al. (2007) applied this method to the rocks from the Shimanto belt and reported a correlation between paleotemperature and the degree of development of the pressure solution. Pressure solution is intensely developed in the underplated tectonic mélange due to higher paleotemperature.

We confirmed that the pressure solution seams are developed in the argillaceous part in the samples from the Kumage complex and the Kadokurasaki complex. The pressure solution seam is sparsely distributes and often develops around the boundary of sandy and muddy portion, which reflects the localization of shear. In the samples of slumping from the Kadokurasaki complex, thin sandstone layer of several tens of μm folds tightly and the black pressure solution seams were observed at the inner hinges of the folds. Chemical composition mapping by electron probe microanalyzer reveals positive anomaly at these black seams, supporting pressure solution. Principal component analysis of the chemical composition data yielded principal components with major loading not only on Si component but also on Ti. The isocon method requires an immobile element as a reference, which are often being Ti, Al or Zr, empirically. Our results confirmed that only Ti is capable of being the immobile reference and supports the validity of the work by KAWABATA et al. (2007).

5. Summary

The argillaceous rocks from the Shimanto belt in Tanega-shima island is weakly metamorphosed, dense and occur well-developed cleavages, suggesting to be shales. Although relatively higher metamorphic degree, these rocks crop out closer to the trench than the other regions in the Shimanto belt, implying different source of heat other than subduction burial. One possibility would be intrusive rocks occurring sporadically in Tanega-shima or huge granite body in Yaku-shima. As these thermal effects must promote the development of pressure solution, further study of quantifying volume change via whole rock chemical composition analysis would help revealing geological evolution around the Osumi islands.

References

FUKUDA, Y. and SAKAI, T. 1993. Sedimentary facies and paleocurrent of Kumage Group, Tanega-shima. Abst. Annl. Meet. Sedimentological Soc. Japan 52. (in Japanese)

GRANT, J.A. 1986. The Isocon Diagram; A simple solution to gresens equation for Metasomatic alteration. Econ. Geol. 81: 1976–1982.

GRESENS, R.L. 1967. Composition-volume relationships of metasomatism. Chemical geology 2: 47–65.

HANZAWA, S. 1934. Geology and geomorphology of Tanega-shima, J. Geol. Soc. Japan 41: 408–410. (in Japanese)

HAYASAKA, S. 1985. Yaku-shima, In: KIZAKI (ed.), Geology of Ryukyu Arc., pp. 29–34. Okinawa Times, Naha. (in Japanese)

HAYASAKA, S., FUKUDA, Y. and HAYAMA, A. 1980. Discovery of molluscan fossils and the paleoenvironmental aspects of the Kumage Group in Tanega-shima,

south Kyushu, Japan. Prof. Saburo Kanno Mem. Vol., 59–70.
HAYASAKA, S., OKADA, H., FUKUDA, Y. and KOJIMA, M. 1983. Geology of Tanega-shima, Field trip guide. Annl. Meeti. Geol. Soc. Japan 90: 113–134. (in Japanese)
KAWABATA, K., TANAKA, H. and KIMURA, G. 2007. Mass transfer and pressure solution in deformed shale of accretionary complex: examples from the Shimanto Belt, southwestern Japan. J. Struct. Geol. 29: 697–711.
KIKUKAWA, A., KOTAKE, N. and KAMEO, K. 2014. Geology and age constraint of the Nishino-omote Formation, Kumage Group, in the northern part of Tanega-shima Island, Kagoshima Prefecture, SW Japan. Abst. Annl. Meet. Geol. Soc. Japan 121. (in Japanese)
KITAMURA, Y. and KIMURA, G. 2012. Dynamic role of tectonic mélange during interseismic process of plate boundary mega earthquakes. Tectonophysics 568–569: 39–52. doi:10.1016/j.tecto.2011.07.008
KITAMURA, Y., SATO, K., IKESAWA, E., IKEHARA-OHMORI, K., KIMURA, G., KONDO, H., UJIIE, K., ONISHI, C.T., KAWABATA, K., HASHIMOTO, Y., MUKOYOSHI, H. and MASAGO, H. 2005. Mélange and its seismogenic roof décollement: A plate boundary fault rock in the subduction zone - An example from the Shimanto Belt, Japan. Tectonics 24: 1–15.
KIZAKI, K. 1978. Tectonics of the Ryukyu Island Arc. J. Phys. Earth, 26 (suppl): 301–307. (in Japanese)
KUWAZURU, J. and NAGATSU, M. 2007. Paleogene radiolarians from the Kumage group in Northern Tanega-shima Island, Kagoshima Prefecture, Japan. 26: 1–11. (in Japanese)
OKADA, H., OKABE, K., SUZUKI, K. and NAKASEKO, K. 1982. Radiolarian fossil assemblages of Kumage Group (Shimanto Belt) in Tanega-shima, Southwest Japan, News Osaka Micropaleont. Spec. Vol. 5, pp. 409–413. (in Japanese with English abstract)
OKADA, H. and WHITAKER, J. H. 1979. Sand volcanoes of the Palaeogene Kumage Group, Tanega-shima, southwest Japan. J. Geol. Soc. Japan 85: 187–196.
SAITO, M., KAWAKAMI, S. and OGASAWARA, M. 2007. Establishment of stratigraphic framework of the Shimanto accretionary complex in Yaku-shima Island, Japan, based on newly found Eocene radiolarian fossils. J. Geol. Soc. Japan 113(6): 266–269. (in Japanese with English abstract)
SAKAI, T. 2010. Southern Shimanto subbelt, Geological Society of Japan (eds.), Regional geology of Japan, 8, Kyushu-Okinawa region, Asakura Pub. Co., Ltd., 141–149. (in Japanese).
SAKAI, T. 1980. Mode of occurrence and origin of greenstones in the Shimanto Terrain in Tanega-shima and Yku-shima islands, Ryukyu Arc. Geol. Studies Ryukyu Island 5: 27–37. (in Japanese with English abstract)
SAKAI, T. 1992. Northern Shimanto Belt-Northeast area, Geology of Japan, 9, Kyushu area, pp. 70–75, Kyoritu Pub., Tokyo. (in Japanese).
SUZUKI, K., NAKASEKO, K. and OKADA, H. 1983. Stratigraphy, structure and age of the Kumage Group, 86th Abst. Annl. Meet. Geol. Soc. Japan, 134. (in Japanese)

Chapter 15
Black Fly of the Osumi Islands

Yasushi OTSUKA

Black flies belong to the family Simuliidae of the order Diptera. 2204 and 76 living species of black flies were recorded in the world and Japan, respectively (ADLER and CROSSKEY 2016). Female adults suck blood of birds and mammals including human for producing their eggs. They are found in any location in which running freshwater streams or rivers suitable for the habitat of their aquatic stages (egg, larva and pupa) are available. The blood-sucking habits of female black flies are responsible for considerable deleterious effects on humans and their economic welfare (CROSSKEY 1990).

The medical and socioeconomic impacts associated with black flies include reduced levels of tourism, the death of domesticated birds and mammals, and the transmission of viral, protozoan and filarial diseases (ADLER et al. 2004). In particular, black flies are well known as vectors of *Onchocerca volvulus* (LEUCKART 1893), the causative filarial species of human onchocerciasis or 'river blindness' endemic in Africa and Central and South America (CROSSKEY 1990). Although such notorious black fly-borne diseases are absent in Japan, in 1989 a case of zoonotic onchocerciasis was first reported in Oita, Kyushu, Japan. Zoonotic onchocerciasis, which is caused by *Onchocerca* species of animal origin, was considered to be very rare; only four cases had been reported prior to 1989, each from Canada, Switzerland, Ukraine and the U.S.A. From 1990 to January 2012, 15 more cases of zoonotic onchocerciasis were reported. These include one from Albania, one from Austria, one from Hungary, one from Kuwait, one from Turkey, and two from the U.S.A., eight (one unpublished and four published cases from Oita, one published case from Hiroshima, and two unpublished cases from each of Hiroshima and Shimane, in the southwest of Honshu) from Japan (TAKAOKA et al. 2012).

By contrast with human onchocerciasis, in which microfilariae produced from gravid female worms cause severe dermal and ocular lesions, zoonotic onchocerciasis is in general caused by a single immature adult female or male worm and thus no microfilariae are produced. However, despite the absence of the conspicuous clinical symptoms caused by microfilariae, conjunctivitis and other ocular lesions caused by an invading adult worm in the ocular or periocular tissue regions (ocular zoonotic onchocerciasis), or a subcutaneous nodule formed around the worm in various parts of the body, can be of clinical importance. The disease is diagnosed by detecting

Table 1. *Onchocerca* species and their host animal in Japan.

Onchocerca species	Host animals
O. dewittei japonica	wild boar (*Sus scrofa*)
O. takaokai	wild boar (*S. scrofa*)
O. lienalis	cattle (*Bos taurus*)
Onchocerca sp. sensu TAKAOKA & BAIN, 1990	cattle (*B. taurus*)
O. eberhardi	sika deer (*Cervus nippon*)
O. skrjabini	sika deer (*C. nippon*), Japanese serrow (*Capricornis crispus*)
O. suzukii	Japanese serrow (*C. crispus*)

an *Onchocerca* worm or its parts in ocular tissue or a resected subcutaneous nodule. However, specific identification based on morphological characteristics is not easy because in most cases only small parts of a worm are available. *Onchocerca gutturosa* NEUMANN, 1910, a common filarialparasite of cattle, and *Onchocerca cervicalis* (STILES 1902), a common parasite of the horse, have been reported as suspected causes of cases identified in Europe and North America. *Onchocerca jakutensis* (GUBANOW 1964), a parasite of deer, was identified by DNA analysis in the case from Austria, and *Onchocerca lupi* RODONAJA, 1967, a parasite of canids, was suspected in the case from Albania and confirmed in the case from Turkey.

A recent study shows that *O. lupi* is responsible for ocular zoonotic onchocerciasis. By contrast, the causative *Onchocerca* species for all nine cases found in Japan was demonstrated to be *Onchocerca dewittei japonica* UNI et al., 2001, a new subspecies from wild boar (*Sus scrofa* LINNAEUS 1758), although theaetiology of the first case was originally suspected to implicate *O. cervicalis* or *O. gutturosa* and that in the second case to implicate *O. gutturosa* (TAKAOKA et al. 2012). Black fly is the vector of the *Onchocerca* species. And the vectors of other species of *Onchocerca* known or newly found in wild boar, cattle, sikadeer (*Cervus nippon* TEMMINCK, 1838) and Japanese serow [*Capricornis crispus* (TEMMINCK, 1845)], all of which have the potential to act as causative agents of zoonotic onchocerciasis in Japan (Table 1). In this chapter, characteristics of the distribution of black fly in the Osumi Islands, the blood sucking damage of blackfly, and the *Onchocerca* species possibly transmitted by black fly are described.

2. Distribution of black fly in the Osumi Islands

In the Osumi Islands, 9 species of black fly are distributed, and are belong to genus *Simulium* LATREILLE s. l. (Table 2). *Simulium aureohirtum* BRUNETTI, 1911, *S. mie* OGATA and SASA, 1954, *S. uchidai* (TAKAHASI 1950) belong to subgenus *Nevermannia* ENDERLEIN. *Simulium arakawae* MATSUMURA, 1915, *S. bidentatum* (SHIRAKI 1935), *Simulium daisense* (TAKAHASI 1950), *S. japonicum* MATSUMURA, 1931, *S. quinquestriatum* (SHIRAKI 1935) and *S. rufibasis* BRUNETTI, 1911 belong to the subgenus *Simulium* Latreille s. str.

Five islands (Kuro-shima Is., Take-shima Is., Kuchinoerabu-jima Is., Yaku-shima Is. and Tanega-shima Is.) are known for habitats of black fly (TAKAOKA 2002, NODA 2011b, Table 3). *Simlulim daisense* was recently collected at Ohkawada river in Tanega-shima Is. (OTSUKA 2015, Fig. 1). This is the first in the Osumi Is., and is the southernmost record. *Simulium uchidai* and *S. arakawae* in Yaku-shima Is. are also the southernmost records. The Watase line, which lies between the Tokara Islands, forms a boundary between the Palearctic and Oriental regions. The Watase line might reflect that the Osumi Islands are southernmost for the

Table 2. Species of black fly in the Osumi Islands.

Simulium (*Nevermannia*) *aureohirtum* BRUNETTI, 1911

Simulium (*Nevermannia*) *mie* OGATA and SASA, 1954

Simulium (*Nevermannia*) *uchidai* (TAKAHASI, 1950)

Simulium (*Simulium*) *arakawae* MATSUMURA, 1915

Simulium (*Simulium*) *bidentatum* (SHIRAKI, 1935)

Simulium (*Simulium*) *daisense* (TAKAHASI, 1950)

Simulium (Simulium) *japonicum* MATSUMURA, 1931

Simulium (*Simulium*) *quinquestriatum* (SHIRAKI, 1935)

Simulium (*Simulium*) *rufibasis* BRUNETTI, 1911

Fig. 1. Ohkawada river in Tanega-shima Is.

Table 3. Distribution of black fly in the Osumi Islands.

	Kuro-shima Is.	Take-shima Is.	Kuchinoerabu-jima Is.	Yaku-shima Is.	Tanega-shima Is.
S. aureohirtum				+	+
S. mie				+	+
S. uchidai	+	+	+	+	+
S. arakawae				+	+
S. bidentatum		+		+	+
S. daisense					+
S. japonicum	+		+	+	+
S. quinquestriatum					+
S. rufibasis				+	

species. *Simulium quinquestriatum* and *S. rufibasis* are the southernmost records in Japan, and are also distributed in Aisa. *Simulium quinquestriatum* is known in Taiwan, China, Korea, Thailand and Vietnam, and was first recorded using specimens of Taiwan. Recent analysis using DNA sequences implies that *S. quinquestriatum* of Taiwan and Japan are separated enough for different species, although those are similar morphologically (OTSUKA unpublished data). To clarify the species status, specimens of *S. quinquestriatum* from other regions should be examine carefully. *Simulium rufibasis* is much distributed in India, Burma, Taiwan, China, Korea, Nepal, Pakistan, Taiwan, Thailand and Vietnam, and is also need to confirm the species status. Like *S. quinquestriatu*, cryptic species occasionally occurs in species distributed widely. As the Osumi Islands is the edge of the Palearctic regions, attention should be paid to specis of the Osumi Islands.

Yaku-shima Is. has many high mountains with altitude of 1,000 m or higher. The highest peak reaches 1,936 m, which is higher than that of the main island of Kyushu. Yaku-shima Is. is thought to have been connected to the main island of Kyushu about 20,000 years ago, as the sea level fell by more than 120 m. In mountain areas of Kumamoto Prefecture in the main island of Kyushu, species of genus *Prosimulium* ROUBAUD, which is common in Holarcric, is distributed. Kumamoto Prefecture is southernmost in Japan for genus *Prosimulium*. I have been suspecting the possibility that genus *Prosimulium* exists in the

Fig. 2. Inokuchi river in Kuro-shima Is.

high mountains in Yaku-shima Is. I hope surveys will be done at the snow mountains of Yaku-shima Is. in March or April.

3. Biting Damage by black fly

At Kuro-shima Is. in Mishima village, the damage caused by black fly is severe. Although two species, *S. japonicum* and *S. uchidai*, are known in Kuro-shima Is. (Talble 3), only *S. japonicum* bites human. To reduce the damages, insecticides are regularly applied into rivers in which larvae of black flies live (Fig. 2). If the river flows smoothly, the effect of the insecticide can be expected sufficiently. But if there is dirt such as fallen leaves in the rivers, or the rivers becomes underground flow, the insecticide will be adsorbed and the effect will decrease rapidly. Also, when there is a large pool in the rivers, the insecticide concentration drops rapidly. Therefore, in using insecticides, it is necessary to thoroughly monitor the state of the rivers. In addition, the situation of the rivers varies according to the season, the amount of water increases during the rainy season, and the number of black fly increases due to the river extending upstream. For this reason, it is insufficient to just input a certain amount of insecticide at a fixed place. The workers, who use the insecticides, must judge the situation of the rivers and make appropriate adjustments. The rivers of Kuro-shima Is. are steep, and there are many places where it is not easy to go back to the rivers by trees, bamboo etc. These problems make the work of applying the insecticides tough.

In Kuro-shima Is., Mishima village does not contract with a specific company for applying the insecticides, but entrusts it to the youth association including school teachers. This is a good method to solve regional problems by themselves. Dr. Shinichi NODA (Research Center for the Pacific Islands, Kagoshima University) and Dr. Hideki SATO (Nippon Environmental Sanitation Center) instructed the control of black fly, and evaluated the effect of the insecticides. In July 2009, they taught 18 members of the youth association who worked for using the insecticides about water flow measurement of the rivers, method of using insecticide and etc. When Drs. NODA and SATO visited Kuro-shima Is. again, they found that the control of black fly by the youth association was highly improved, and that the control was sufficiently effective (NODA 2011a).

Although the control of black fly in Kuro-shima Is. continued, it was surprising that a large number of blackflies occurred sometime. Dr. NODA visited only once in a year to Kuro-shima Is. for the instruction and evaluation. Therefore, he was not sure whether the use of the insecticides was properly done throughout the year or not. When Dr. NODA had an opportunity to visit Kuro-shima Is. for other work in September 2010, he asked a school teacher about the control of black fly. The teacher said that insecticides were not used after April this year. As Dr. NODA was worried, the occurrence of the current black fly damage was simply due to not using the insecticides into the rivers. During the rainy season, damage of black fly bites increase. It is conceivable that as the temperature rises, the generation cycle of black fly becomes shorter, and as the precipitation increases, the river extends upstream and spreads habitats of larvae of black fly. Therefore, in order to reduce the damage in the summer season, it is important to implement countermeasure against April and May. Periodic change of the school teacher in April occurs every year, and it was necessary to consider how to implement the blunt countermeasure in this period (NODA 2011a).

The huge number of black fly made unable to work outside the house. However, continuous uses of insecticide make worry about the effect to the nature. So, when the damage of black fly is at low level, we have to seek alternative method to suppress the black fly to maintain the community

Fig. 3. Collection site near Kigen-Sugi in Yaku-shima Is.

Fig. 4. Adult females of *S. japonicum* (left) and *S. rufibasis* (right).

and nature of the islands.

Yaku-shima Is. has many rivers suitable for habitats of larvae of black fly, but severe damage of black fly is not reported. When a collection of adults of black fly was made near Kigen-Sugi in Yaku-shima Is. by human bait trap with car engine in October 2014 (Fig. 3), 25 females of *S. rufibasis* and 23 females of *S. japonicum* were captured within about 4 hours (OTSUKA 2015, Fig. 4). This suggests that in Yaku-shima Is., not only *S. japonicum*, *S. rufibasis* was also important species attracted to human. The collection site was at an altitude of 700 m. In Yaku-shima Is., *S. japonicum* and *S. rufibasis* mainly appear in high land, the two species were not so much in low land. This is one reason that damages of black fly don't occur so much in Yaku-shima Is.. Most resident houses are in low land. But, I heard from some researchers worked in the forest in Yaku-shima Is. that they were attacked by black flies. It means that tourists and workers who go in high land must take care of black fly using repellents or hiding their skin with long sleeves. In Kuro-shima Is., resident houses are near the rivers where larvae of *S. japonicum* live. This situation is similar to Nakano-shima Is. and Kuchino-shima Is in the Tokara Islands where severe damages of black fly occur. *Simulium japonicum* is also in Tanega-shima Is. But, Tanega-shima Is. doesn't have many rivers for habitats of larvae of *S. japonicum*. Probably for the reason, damage of black fly is not known in Tanega-shima Is.

Onchocerca species in black flies of the Osumi Islands is not surveyed yet. Different from the main islands of Japan, there is no wild boar in the Osumi Islands. It means that onchocerciasis by *O. dewittei japonica* doesn't occur in the Osumi Islands. But, each island has cattle which have known to have some *Onchocerca* species in the main islands of Japan. And, Yakushika, a subspecies of Japanese deer, exists in Yaku-shima Is. As Yakushika may have different *Onchocerca* species from Japanese deer, *Onchocerca* species and their vector in the Osumi Islands must be clarified.

References

ADLER, P. H. and CROSSKEY, R. W. 2016. World blackflies (Diptera: Simuliidae): A Comprehensive revision of the taxonomic and geographical inventory [2016]. 126 pp., http://entweb.clemson.edu/biomia/pdfs/blackflyinventory.pdf (Accessed on 15 November 2016).

ADLER, P. H., CURRIE, D. C. and Wood, D. M. 2004. The black flies (Simuliidae) of North America. xv + 941 pp., Cornell University Press, Ithaca, New York.

CROSSKEY, R. W. 1990. The natural history of blackflies. John Wiley & Sons Inc., Chichester.

NODA, S. 2011a. Control of blackfly in Kuro Island, Mishima Village, Kagoshima Prefecture. Occasional papers, Research Center for the Pacific Islands, Kagoshima University 51: 16–19. (in Japanese with English abstract)

NODA, S. 2011b. Survey of medical insects and arachnids on Kuchinoerabu Island, Yaku-shima Town, Kagoshima Prefecture. Occasional papers, Research Center for the Pacific Islands, Kagoshima University 51: 76–79. (in Japanese with English abstract)

OTSUKA, Y. 2015. A survey of filarial parasites transmitted by blackflies in the Osumi Islands. Occasional papers, Research Center for the Pacific Islands, Kagoshima University 59: 29–31. (in Japanese with English abstract)

TAKAOKA, H. 2002. Review on the classification, distribution and ecology of the black flies (Diptera: Simuliidae) of the Nansei Islands in Japan, with techniques for collection, slide-preparation, microscopic observation, and identification of adult, pupal and larval black flies. Medical Entomology and Zoology 53 (Suppl. 2): 55–80. (in Japanese with English abstract)

TAKAOKA, H., FUKUDA, M., OTSUKA, Y., AOKI, C., UNI, S. and BAIN, O. 2012. Blackfly vectors of zoonotic onchocerciasis in Japan. Medical and Veterinary Entomology 26(4): 372–378.

Chapter 16
Seaweeds and Coastal Environment in the Osumi Islands

Ryuta TERADA and Yuki WATANABE

1. Introduction

Seaweeds are marine benthic and photosynthetic organisms commonly found in coastal areas, especially in the rocky shores. They serve a significant role in the coastal ecosystem as primary producers and habitats for fish and invertebrate assemblages. Seaweed is a general term for the benthic marine macroalgae that includes the red (Rhodophyceae), brown (Phaeophyceae) and green algae (Ulvophyceae); all of which belong to the Kingdom Protista (DAWS 1998, GRAHAM and WILCOX 2000). In general, seaweeds inhabit shallow coastal waters, and are strongly influenced by various environmental factors including irradiance (sunlight), temperature, nutrients, and wave motion. Irradiance is a crucial factor in the photosynthesis of these macroalgae, and so in their vertical distribution in the sea. Likewise, seawater temperature is important for the growth and survival of each species group, and is also considered a determining factor in their geographical distribution.

Kagoshima Prefecture is located in both the southern part of Kyushu Island and the island chain of the northern Ryukyu Archipelago, covering a distance of approximately 600 km from north to south (32°20′N to 27°N). This region is regarded as the ecotone of temperate and tropical / subtropical seaweeds distribution; hence, algal species in this region are subjected to both climate fluctuations. Temperate species dominate the Kagoshima proper (Kyushu); while tropical / subtropical species are distributed in the Amami Islands of middle Ryukyu Archipelago, and extend further south. The Osumi Islands comprise 6 inhabited islands including Tanega-shima Island and Yaku-shima Island; and are located in the northern end of the Ryukyu Archipelago. The islands are geographically close to the southern part of Kyushu Island; however, the flora of seaweeds is rather similar to those in Amami Islands with subtropical climate.

In Kagoshima Prefecture, coastal surface seawater temperature in summer (August to early September) reaches around 28°C, with little temperature variation within the prefecture. However, in winter, there is a characteristic latitudinal gradient in seawater temperature along the Osumi and Amami Islands, with a difference of 5°C. In fact, surface seawater temperature in Kagoshima Bay (Kyushu) decreases to ~15°C in February; while in Osumi and Amami Islands, they sit at ~18 and 20 °C, respectively (Kagoshima Prefecture Fisheries Technology and Development Center 2017). Seawater temperature in mainland Kagoshima is different from those in the remote islands, despite belonging in the same prefecture.

Coastal seawater temperature in the Osumi Islands is influenced by the warm Kuroshio Current (Japan Current) that flows along this region (Fig. 1). The Kuroshio Current occurs off the east coast of the Philippines, and flows offshore on the west coast of the Ryukyu Archipelago including the Amami Islands. Thereafter, it crosses the archipelago off the south coast of Yaku-shima and Tanega-shima islands, and enters the Pacific Ocean (NAKAMURA et al. 2015). Because of the Kuroshio Current, relatively warm winter seawater temperatures enable the survival of tropical / subtropical seaweeds in the Osumi Islands, which marks the world's northernmost distribution for these species.

2. Seaweeds in the Osumi Islands

The exact number of seaweed and seagrass species growing in the Osumi Islands is still unknown;

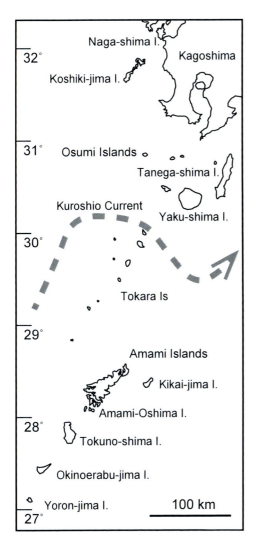

Fig. 1. Map of the islands in Kagoshima Prefecture showing the Kuroshio Current (dashed arrow).

Fig. 2. Common species of *Sargassum* (Sargassaceae) in the Osumi Islands. A, *Sargassum ilicifolium*; B, *Sargassum polyporum*.

however, more than 200 species of seaweeds have been reported in this region (SHINMURA 1990, Terada and Suzuki 2011a, b). In the Kagoshima proper (Kyushu), most common seaweeds that compose high density communities are species of *Sargassum* (Sargassaceae), *Undaria pinnatifida* (Alariaceae; Wakame in Japanese) and *Ecklonia radicosa* (= *Eckloniopsis radicosa*, Lessoniaceae; Antokume in Japanese). Meanwhile, no *U. pinnatifida* is found in the Osumi Islands, as well as in the Ryukyu Archipelago (WATANABE *et al.* 2014). *E. radicosa* that was previously observed in the Osumi Islands as its southern distributional limit has disappeared from this region in the past two decades (KOMAZAWA *et al.* 2015, TERADA *et al.* 2016). Although species of *Sargassum*, particularly the tropical / subtropical *S. ilicifolium* (Fig. 2A) and *S. polyporum* are common (Fig. 2B), they have also decreased in the past two decades (TERADA unpublished data); thereby suggesting a serious cause for concern. Unfortunately, the ecology of these seaweed species has not been fully elucidated. Knowledge on this aspect, including their adaptation to the prevailing environment is essential for the conservation of algal communities.

Relatively small tropical / subtropical species also occur in the Osumi Islands. Algal species such as *Asparagopsis taxiformis* (Bonnemaisoniaceae; Fig. 3A), *Chondria ryukyuensis* (Rhodomelaceae;

Fig. 3B), *Dictyota divaricata* (Dictyotaceae; Fig. 3C), *Caulerpa webbiana* (Caulerpaceae; Fig. 3D), *Halimeda discoidea* (Halimedaceae; Fig. 3E) and *Chlorodesmis fastigiata* (Udoteaceae; Fig. 3F) are found attached in rocks in the intertidal and shallow subtidal zones. Seaweeds are also observed at depths of 30–50 m offshore of Mageshima Island suggesting the relatively clear ocean water in the region that enables irradiance to penetrate such depths in the lower subtidal zone (TANAKA 1963; YAMADA *et al.* 2013; PINTO *et al.* 2017). The maximum irradiance at depths of 35 m is reported to be less than 200 μmol photons m^{-2} sec^{-1}. Photosynthetic studies of subtidal species from this region have been conducted to elucidate their adaptation to low irradiance environment

Fig. 3. Common species small algae in the Osumi Islands. A, *Asparagopsis taxiformis* (Bonnemaisoniaceae); B, *Chondria ryukyuensis* (Rhodomelaceae); C, *Dictyota divaricata* (Dictyotaceae); D, *Caulerpa webbiana* (Caulerpaceae); E, *Halimeda discoidea* (Halimedaceae); F, and *Chlorodesmis fastigiata* (Udoteaceae).

Fig. 4. Edible algae in the Osumi Islands. A, *Pyropia yamadae* (Bangiaceae); B, *Pyropia dentata* (Bangiaceae); C, *Pyropia tanegashimensis* (Bangiaceae); D, *Monostroma nitidum* (Gomontiaceae).

(TERADA *et al.* 2016, BORLONGAN *et al.* in press).

In the Osumi Islands, a typical coral reef (fringing reef) is rare in the region, with shores offering rocky substrata to seaweeds and tiny turf algae. The coast is often influenced by heavy waves. While estuarine areas with muddy bottoms are widespread in the Ryukyu Islands, they are limited in the Osumi Islands, particularly in the islands of Yaku-shima, Take-shima, Io-jima, Kuro-shima and Kuchinoerabu-jima.

3. Utilization of seaweed

Seaweeds are indispensable in Japanese dietary culture, as they are most often present at every meal as salads or in soup (OHNO and LARGO 1998). Such edible seaweeds include some local species of *Pyropia* (Bangiaceae; Nori in Japanese), like *P. yamadae* (Tsukushi-amanori in Japanese; Fig. 4A), *P. dentata* (Oni-amanori in Japanese; Fig. 4B) and *P. tanegashimensis* (Tanegashima-amanori in Japanese; Fig. 4C), as well as the green alga, *Monostroma nitidum* (Gomontiaceae; *Hitoegusa* in Japanese; Fig. 4D). While a lot of them are observed during winter through early summer, they are harvested by local inhabitants for commercial use and regional consumption in the islands. Protection and management of the coastal environment is indeed important not only for the sustainable use of this important regional resource, but also for the conservation of natural communities.

References

BORLONGAN, I. A., NISHIHARA, G. N., SHIMADA, S. and TERADA, R. 2017. Photosynthetic performance of the red alga *Solieria pacifica* (Solieriaceae) from two different depths in the sublittoral waters of Kagoshima, Japan. Journal of Applied Phycology (in press).

DAWS, C. J. 1998. Marine Botany. Second Edition. 480 pp., Wiley, New York.

GRAHAM, L., E. and WILCOX, L. W. 2000. Algae. 640 pp., Prentice-Hall, Upper Saddle River, New Jersey.

Kagoshima Prefecture Fisheries Technology and Development Center 2017. Status of the coastal seawater temperature. http://kagoshima.suigi.jp/ (Accessed on 15 January 2017; in Japanese).

KOMAZAWA, I., SAKANISHI, Y. and TANAKA, J. 2015. Temperature requirements for growth and maturation of the warm temperate kelp *Eckloniopsis radicosa* (Laminariales, Phaeophyta). Phycological Research 63 (1): 64–71.

NAKAMURA, H. 2015. The Kuroshio. Its physical aspect and roles in Kagoshima's nature and culture. In: KAWAI, K., TERADA, R. and KUWAHARA, S. (eds), The Islands of Kagoshima, Culture, Society, Industry and Nature, Second Edition, pp. 118–127. Hokuto Shobo Publishing, Tokyo.

OHNO, M. and LARGO, D. B. 1998. The seaweed resources of Japan. In: Critchley, A. T. and Ohno, M. (eds), Seaweed resources of the world, pp. 1–14. Japan International Cooperation Agency, Yokosuka.

SHINMURA, I. 1990. List of marine algae of Kagoshima Prefecture. Mem. Kagoshima Fish. Exp. Sta. 13: 1–112. (in Japanese)

PINTO, S. K., TERADA, R. and HORIGUCHI, T. 2017. *Testudodinium magnum* sp. nov. (Dinophyceae), a novel marine sand-dwelling dinoflagellate from subtropical Japan. Phycologia 56 (2): 136–146.

TANAKA, T. 1963. Studies on some marine algae from southern japan V. Mem. Fac. Fish. Kagoshima Univ. 12: 75–91.

TERADA, R. and SUZUKI, T. 2011a. Marine algal flora and its community structure of Kuroshima Island, Mishima Village, Kagoshima, Japan. Kagoshima University Research Center for the Pacific Islands Occasional Papers 51: 6–15. (in Japanese with English Abstract)

TERADA, R. and SUZUKI, T. 2011b. Preliminary study of benthic marine algae from Kuchinoerabu Island, Kagoshima, Japan. Kagoshima University Research Center for the Pacific Islands Occasional Papers 51: 69–75. (in Japanese with English Abstract)

TERADA, R., SHIKADA, S., WATANABE, Y., NAKAZAKI, Y., MATSUMOTO, K., KOZONO, J., SAINO, N. and NISHIHARA, G. N. 2016. Effect of PAR and temperature on the photosynthesis of Japanese alga, *Ecklonia radicosa* (Laminariales), based on field and laboratory measurements. Phycologia 55 (2): 178–186.

WATANABE, Y., NISHIHARA, G. N., TOKUNAGA, S. and TERADA, R. 2014. The effect of irradiance and temperature responses and the phenology of a native alga, *Undaria pinnatifida* (Laminariales), at the southern limit of its natural distribution in Japan. Journal of Applied Phycology 26 (6): 2405–2415.

YAMADA, N., TERADA, R., TANAKA, A. and HORIGUCHI, T. 2013. *Diplospina angelus* gen. et sp. nov. (Dinophyceae), a new sand-dwelling dinoflagellate from seafloor off Mageshima island, Japan. Journal of Phycology 49 (3): 555–569.

The Osumi Islands
Culture, Society, Industry and Nature

2017年3月　初版1刷発行

編集者　　河合　渓
　　　　　寺田　竜太
　　　　　桑原　季雄

鹿児島大学国際島嶼教育研究センター
〒890-8580　鹿児島市郡元1-21-24
TEL 099-285-7394　FAX 099-285-6197

発行所　　㈲北斗書房
〒132-0024　東京都江戸川区一之江8-3-2
TEL 03-3674-5241　FAX 03-3674-5244

印刷所　三報社印刷㈱　定価1,600円＋税